Nutrient Concentrations, Loads, and Yields in the Eucha-Spavinaw Basin, Arkansas and Oklahoma, 2002–09

By Rachel A. Esralew and Robert L. Tortorelli

In cooperation with the City of Tulsa, Oklahoma

Scientific Investigations Report 2010–5119

U.S. Department of the Interior
U.S. Geological Survey

U.S. Department of the Interior
KEN SALAZAR, Secretary

U.S. Geological Survey
Marcia K. McNutt, Director

U.S. Geological Survey, Reston, Virginia: 2010

This and other USGS information products are available at http://store.usgs.gov/
U.S. Geological Survey
Box 25286, Denver Federal Center
Denver, CO 80225

To learn about the USGS and its information products visit http://www.usgs.gov/
1-888-ASK-USGS

Suggested citation:
Esralew, R.A., and Tortorelli, R.L., 2010, Nutrient concentrations, loads, and yields in the Eucha-Spavinaw Basin, Arkansas and Oklahoma, 2002–09: U.S. Geological Survey Scientific Investigations Report 2010–5119, 61 p.

Contents

Figures

Tables

Conversion Factors

Multiply	By	To obtain
Length		
mile (mi)	1.609	kilometer (km)
Area		
square mile (mi^2)	2.590	square kilometer (km^2)
Flow rate		
cubic foot per second (ft^3/s)	0.02832	cubic meter per second (m^3/s)
gallon per day (gal/d)	0.003785	cubic meter per day (m^3/d)
million gallons per day (Mgal/d)	0.04381	cubic meter per second (m^3/s)
Mass		
pound (lb)	0.4536	kilogram (kg)
pound per day (lb/d)	0.4536	kilogram per day (kg/d)
pound per year (lb/yr)	0.4536	kilogram per year (kg/yr)
pound per year per square mile [(lb/yr)/ mi^2]	0.1751	kilogram per year per square kilometer [(kg/yr)/mi^2]
ton	0.9072	megagram

Vertical coordinate information is referenced to the North American Vertical Datum of 1988 (NAVD 88).

Horizontal coordinate information is referenced to the North American Datum of 1983 (NAD 83).

Concentrations of chemical constituents in water are given in milligrams per liter (mg/L).

Method detection limit (MDL)—Minimum concentration of a substance that can be measured and reported with 99-percent confidence that the analyte concentration is greater than zero. It is determined from the analysis of a sample in a given matrix containing the analyte (U.S. Environmental Protection Agency, 1997). At the MDL concentration, the risk of a false positive is predicted to be less than or equal to 1 percent (Childress and others, 1999).

Long-term method detection level (LT–MDL)—A detection level derived by determining the standard deviation of a minimum of 24 MDL spike sample measurements over an extended period of time. LT–MDL data are collected on a continuous basis to assess year-to-year variations in the LT–MDL. The LT–MDL controls false positive error. The chance of falsely reporting a concentration at or greater than the LT–MDL for a sample that did not contain the analyte is predicted to be less than or equal to 1 percent (Childress and others, 1999).

Laboratory reporting level (LRL)—Generally equal to twice the yearly determined LT–MDL. The LRL controls false negative error. The probability of falsely reporting a non-detection for a sample that contained an analyte at a concentration equal to or greater than the LRL is predicted to be less than or equal to 1 percent. The value of the LRL will be reported with a "less than" remark code for samples in which the analyte was not detected. These values are reevaluated annually based on the most current quality-control data and may, therefore, change (Childress and others, 1999).

Nutrient Concentrations, Loads, and Yields in the Eucha-Spavinaw Basin, Arkansas and Oklahoma, 2002–09

By Rachel A. Esralew and Robert L. Tortorelli

Abstract

The city of Tulsa, Oklahoma, uses Lake Eucha and Spavinaw Lake in the Eucha-Spavinaw Basin in northwestern Arkansas and northeastern Oklahoma for public water supply. The city has spent millions of dollars over the last decade to eliminate taste and odor problems in the drinking water from the Eucha-Spavinaw system, which may be attributable to blue-green algae. Increases in the algal biomass in the lakes may be attributable to increases in nutrient concentrations in the lakes and in the waters feeding the lakes. The U.S. Geological Survey, in cooperation with the City of Tulsa, investigated and summarized total nitrogen and total phosphorus concentrations in water samples and provided estimates of nitrogen and phosphorus loads, yields, and flow-weighted concentrations during base flow and runoff for two streams discharging to Lake Eucha for the period January 2002 through December 2009. This report updates a previous report that used data from water-quality samples collected from January 2002 through December 2006.

Based on the results from the Mann-Whitney statistical test, unfiltered total nitrogen concentrations were significantly greater in runoff water samples than in base-flow water samples collected from Spavinaw Creek near Maysville and near Cherokee City, Arkansas; Spavinaw Creek near Colcord, Oklahoma, and Beaty Creek near Jay, Oklahoma. Nitrogen concentrations in runoff water samples collected from all stations generally increased with increasing streamflow.

Nitrogen concentrations in base-flow and runoff water samples collected in Spavinaw Creek significantly increased from the station furthest upstream (near Maysville) to the Sycamore station and then significantly decreased from the Sycamore station to the station furthest downstream (near Colcord). Nitrogen concentrations in base-flow and runoff water samples collected from Beaty Creek were significantly less than base-flow and runoff water samples collected from Spavinaw Creek.

Based on the results from the Mann-Whitney statistical test, unfiltered total phosphorus concentrations were significantly greater in runoff water samples than in base-flow water samples for the entire period for most stations, except in water samples collected from Spavinaw Creek near Cherokee City, in which no significant difference was detected for the entire period nor for any season. Phosphorus concentrations in runoff water samples collected from all stations generally increased with increasing streamflow.

Based on results from a multi-stage Kruskal-Wallis statistical test, phosphorus concentrations in base-flow water samples collected from Spavinaw Creek significantly increased from the Maysville station to the Cherokee City station, probably because of discharge from a municipal wastewater-treatment plant between those stations. Phosphorus concentrations significantly decreased downstream from the Cherokee City station to the Colcord station. Phosphorus concentrations in base-flow water samples collected from Beaty Creek were significantly less than phosphorus in base-flow water samples collected from Spavinaw Creek downstream from the Maysville station.

Estimated mean annual nitrogen total and base-flow loads were substantially greater in Spavinaw Creek than in Beaty Creek, and increased downstream from the Maysville station to the Colcord station in Spavinaw Creek. Estimated mean annual phosphorus total loads were greater for the Spavinaw Creek stations from the Cherokee City station to the Colcord station than for the Beaty Creek station, and increased downstream from the Maysville station to the Colcord station in Spavinaw Creek. The runoff component of the mean annual nitrogen total load for Beaty Creek was 88 percent; whereas, for the Spavinaw Creek stations, the range in the runoff component accounted for 67 to 73 percent of the mean annual nitrogen load.

The runoff component of the mean annual phosphorus total load for the Beaty Creek station was 98 percent; whereas, at the Spavinaw Creek stations, the range in the runoff component accounted for 79 to 93 percent of the mean annual phosphorus load. Annual nitrogen and phosphorus total, base-flow, and runoff loads were greatest during the calendar year 2008 and lowest during the calendar year 2006.

Estimated mean annual nitrogen total yields ranged from 6,160 to 8,070 pounds per year per square mile with the greatest yield at the Colcord station and the least yield at the Beaty Creek station.

Estimated mean annual phosphorus total yields ranged from 300 to 620 pounds per year per square mile with greatest the yield at the Beaty Creek station and the least yield at the Maysville station.

Estimated mean flow-weighted nitrogen concentrations at all stations in the basin were about 7 to 10 times greater than the 75th percentile of flow-weighted nitrogen concentrations (0.50 milligram per liter) in other mostly undeveloped basins of the United States. Estimated mean flow-weighted phosphorus concentrations at all stations in the basin were about five to nine times greater than the 75th percentile of flow-weighted phosphorus concentrations (0.037 milligram per liter) in other mostly undeveloped basins of the United States.

Spavinaw Creek and Beaty Creek contributed an estimated mean annual nitrogen total load of 1,681,000 pounds per year, 76 percent of which was transported to Lake Eucha by runoff. Spavinaw Creek and Beaty Creek contributed an estimated mean annual phosphorus total load of 108,390 pounds per year, 91 percent of which was transported to Lake Eucha by runoff.

Introduction

The city of Tulsa, Oklahoma, uses Lake Eucha and Spavinaw Lake in the Eucha-Spavinaw Basin in northwestern Arkansas and northeastern Oklahoma for public water supply (fig. 1). Construction of Spavinaw Dam (U.S. Geological Survey lake-level station at Spavinaw Lake, station identifier 07191300, fig. 1) on Spavinaw Creek began in 1922 and was completed in 1924 (Oklahoma Water Resources Board, 2002). A series of pipelines 60-miles long was constructed to transfer water from the base of Spavinaw Lake Dam to a wastewater-treatment plant in Tulsa. Spavinaw Lake supplied Tulsa with a safe, reliable water supply (Oklahoma Water Resources Board, 2002). In 1950, city officials decided to create an impoundment of Spavinaw Creek four miles upstream from Spavinaw Lake to serve as "an environmental and hydrologic barrier" for Spavinaw Lake to ensure a constant supply of clean water. This second dam came to be known as Eucha Dam (U.S. Geological Survey lake-level station at Lake Eucha, station identifier 07191285, fig. 1) that was finished in 1954 to impound Lake Eucha (fig. 1) (City of Tulsa City Services, 2008a).

The Eucha-Spavinaw system continues to be designated as a system for public water supply as well as for recreation, fish and wildlife, agriculture, and aesthetics (City of Tulsa City Services, 2008b). The Eucha-Spavinaw system provides 59 million gallons per day (Mgal/d) to the Tulsa metropolitan area. During peak demand, the system can produce a maximum of 100 Mgal/d (City of Tulsa City Services, 2008b).

Taste and odor problems in the drinking water have been reported by consumers to the City of Tulsa municipal agency (COT) (City of Tulsa City Services, 2008c). The Tulsa Metropolitan Utility Authority (TMUA) spent millions of dollars from 1998–2005 to eliminate taste and odor problems, likely attributable to the chemicals produced by blue-green algae, notably geosmin, in the drinking water from the Eucha-Spavinaw system (Oklahoma Water Resources Board, 2002;

City of Tulsa City Services, 2008c). Changes in the algal biomass and abundance in the lakes are the result of increases in nutrient concentrations in the tributaries of the lakes (City of Tulsa City Services, 2008c). Elevated nitrogen and phosphorus concentrations promote algae growth in streams (Sharpley, 1995; U.S. Geological Survey, 1999) and accelerate eutrophication of lakes (Daniel and others, 1998; U.S. Geological Survey, 1999). A study of phosphorous loading in this basin by the Oklahoma Conservation Commission report indicated increasing nutrient content of Spavinaw Creek, a main tributary to Lake Eucha (fig. 1), between 1975 and 1995 (Wagner and Woodruff, 1997). Lake Eucha and Spavinaw Lake were nutrient-enriched (phosphorus was the limiting nutrient), and high or excessive levels of algal production were detected in the lakes (Oklahoma Water Resources Board, 2002).

Nitrogen and phosphorus can enter streams in discharges from wastewater-treatment plants (point-source components) and in agricultural and urban runoff (nonpoint-source components) (Oklahoma Water Resources Board, 2002). The main sources of elevated nitrogen and phosphorus concentrations in streams in the Eucha-Spavinaw Basin are from nonpoint sources (notably runoff from fertilized pastures) and point sources (notably wastewater discharge) (Tortorelli, 2008; City of Tulsa, 2010). Pastures fertilized with animal manure or commercial fertilizer probably are substantial sources of nitrogen and phosphorus delivered to the streams in this basin, especially during runoff (Storm and others, 2002).

One possible major contributor of nutrients to the creeks feeding Lake Eucha and Spavinaw Lake is the phosphorous-rich waste produced by commercial poultry raising operations in the watershed. This waste is routinely spread onto fields as fertilizer and can be a source of nitrogen and phosphorous washed into streams as nonpoint-source pollution, which ultimately reaches the water-supply lakes and promotes growth of unwanted algae (Storm and others, 2002). As of 2001, production of 1,500 tons of nitrogen and phosphorous-rich waste in the basin per year was estimated (Tulsa Metropolitan Utility Authority, 2001). As of 2007, the poultry operations in the Eucha-Spavinaw Basin have the capacity to produce more than 160 million birds (U.S. Department of Agriculture, 2009; table 1). More than 84,000 acres were treated with manure in 2002, but this amount was reduced to about 52,000 acres in 2007 (U.S. Department of Agriculture 2004 and 2009, table 1). In 2001, the COT filed suit against several poultry-producing companies. The lawsuit was settled out of court and in 2004 resulted in a substantial reduction in land application of poultry litter (City of Tulsa, 2010). The reduction in litter application may have led to the decrease in treated acres between 2002 and 2007.

Nutrient concentrations in streams vary throughout the year, mainly in response to variation in precipitation and streamflow, and to variation in the timing of fertilizer or manure applications (U.S. Geological Survey, 1999). Nutrient concentrations in streams may be greater during occurrences of high streamflow, especially during spring and summer after fertilizer application. Increased nutrient concentrations were

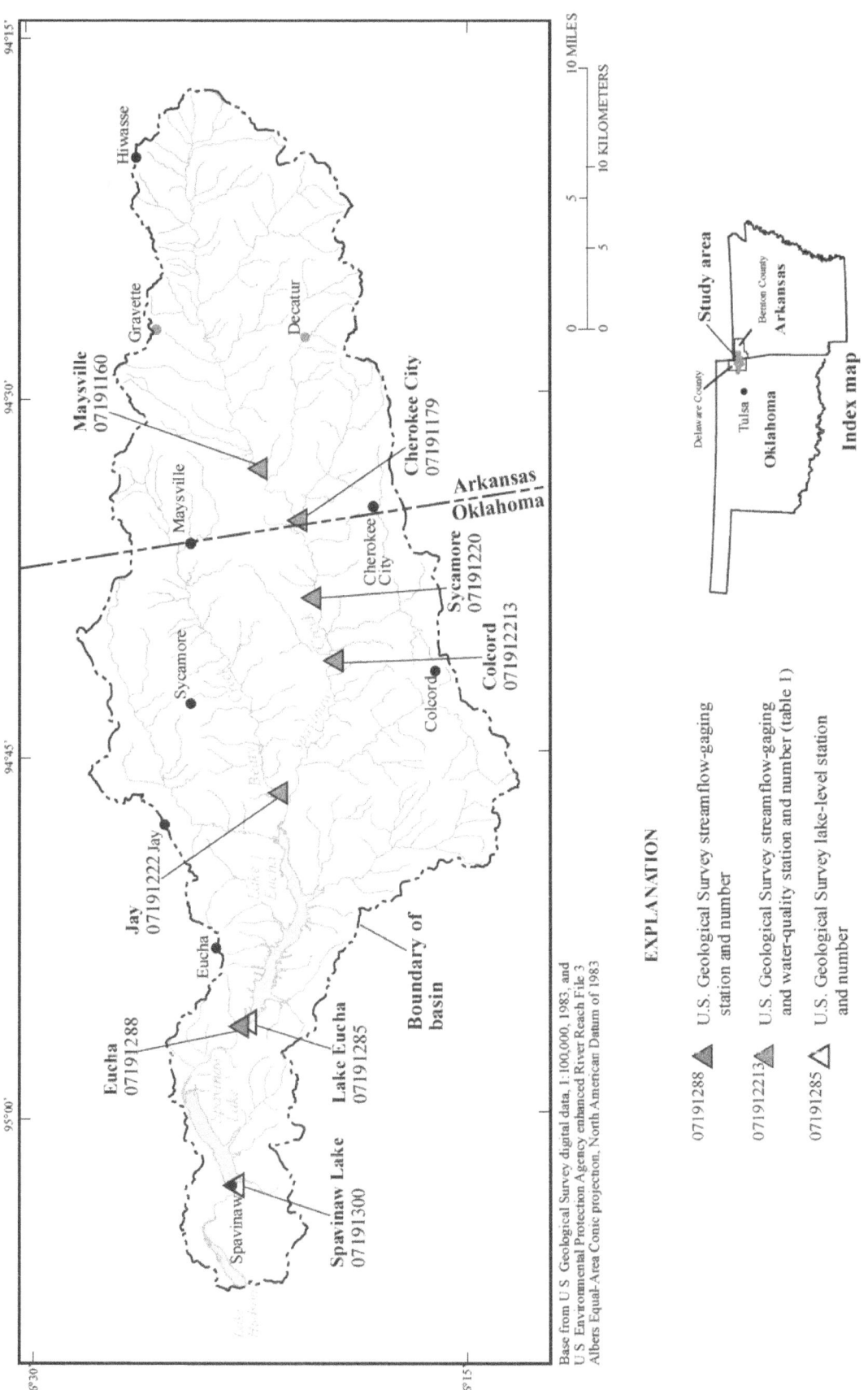

Base from U S Geological Survey digital data, 1:100,000, 1983, and
U S Environmental Protection Agency enhanced River Reach File 3
Albers Equal-Area Conic projection, North American Datum of 1983

EXPLANATION

07191288 ▲ U.S. Geological Survey streamflow-gaging
station and number

071912213▲ U.S. Geological Survey streamflow-gaging
and water-quality station and number (table 1)

07191285 △ U.S. Geological Survey lake-level station
and number

● Town with water-treatment plant that
discharges into streams in the Eucha-
Spavinaw Basin

Figure 1. The Eucha-Spavinaw Basin, Arkansas and Oklahoma, with locations of selected streamflow-gaging water-quality, and lake-level stations in the basin and towns with wastewater-treatment plants that discharge nto streams in the basin.

Table 1.   Estimates of fertilizer application, number of cattle and calves, and number of broilers and other chickens sold for counties in the Eucha-Spavinaw Basin, Arkansas and Oklahoma, 2002 and 2007.

[modified from U.S. Department of Agriculture (2004, 2009)]

County	Percentage of county in drainage basin of Beaty Creek near Jay (station 07191222)	Percentage of county in drainage basin of Spavinaw Creek near Colcord (station 071912213)	Farm-land (acres)	Year	Acres treated with com-mercial fertilizer	Acres treated with manure	Total acres treated	Percent of county area (farms only) treated with fertilizer[1]	Num-ber of cattle and calves	Number of broilers and other chickens sold
Delaware, Okla.	67.4	23.5	282,106	2002	53,185	21,346	74,531	26	74,719	37,154,935
				2007	57,613	17,926	75,539	27	83,197	47,971,853
Benton, Ark.	32.6	76.5	312,646	2002	84,703	62,829	147,532	47	113,588	128,066,609
				2007	57,786	33,779	91,565	29	94,588	116,599,600

[1] Fertilizer application to land other than farms (for example, golf courses or residences) was not included.

detected in streams during seasonal low flows. In particular, nitrogen and phosphorus concentrations may be elevated in streams downstream from urban areas during seasonal low flows when contributions from point sources, such as waste-water treatment plants, are greater relative to streamflow, and dilution is minimal (U.S. Geological Survey, 1999).

Potential means of minimizing eutrophication in the Eucha-Spavinaw Basin include: (a) reduction in the quanti-ties of nutrients running off or seeping into surface water, and (b) control of the ratios of nitrogen and phosphorus in tributaries that deliver these nutrients to the lakes. Nitrogen-to-phosphorus ratios are useful for general guidance as to what nutrient may be most likely to encourage plant growth in sur-face water, but if nutrient concentrations are sufficiently large, then these nutrients may be available for uptake regardless of the ratio. Nitrogen-to-phosphorus ratios of 20 to 1 or greater indicate potential deficiency of phosphorus; whereas, ratios of 10 to 1 or less indicate potential deficiency of nitrogen (United Nations Environmental Programme, 2007). Blue-green algae tend to bloom when phosphorus concentrations are increased relative to nitrogen (Levich, 1996). However, total phosphorus and total nitrogen may not be readily available for uptake, because these constituents may be bound to small colloids or other particles (Jones and Knowlton, 1993).

As of 2010, the USGS has operated five continuous streamflow-gaging and water-quality data collection stations in the Eucha-Spavinaw Basin in Arkansas and Oklahoma: Spavinaw Creek near Maysville, Arkansas; Spavinaw Creek near Cherokee City, Arkansas; Spavinaw Creek near Sycamore, Oklahoma; Spavinaw Creek near Colcord, Okla-homa; and Beaty Creek near Jay, Oklahoma (fig. 1). For the remainder of this report, these stations are referred to as the

Maysville station, Cherokee City station, Sycamore station, and Colcord station on Spavinaw Creek (or collectively as the "Spavinaw Creek stations"), and the Beaty Creek station, respectively.

Historically, water-quality data collection for stations in the Eucha-Spavinaw Basin has been on a fixed monthly schedule. Most of the water samples were collected during base flow (nonrunoff) because runoff events are variable and infrequent. For this report, all samples are water samples. Because of the lack of runoff samples collected, calculations using historic data may have underestimated true nutrient con-centrations, loads, and yields. In July 2001, the U.S. Geologi-cal Survey (USGS), in cooperation with COT, supplemented scheduled monthly water-quality sampling with six targeted runoff samplings per year for five stations to better determine water quality over a broader range of streamflows in the basin. The period 2002–09 encompasses a period where the runoff sampling protocol was in effect. The USGS, in cooperation with COT, investigated and summarized nitrogen and phos-phorus concentrations and provided estimates of nitrogen and phosphorus loads, yields, and flow-weighted concentrations in the Eucha-Spavinaw Basin from January 2002 through December 2009.

Purpose and Scope

The purpose of this report is to summarize nutrient concentrations, loads, and yields in the Eucha-Spavinaw Basin from January 2002 through December 2009. Specifically, total nitrogen and total phosphorus concentrations in water samples are summarized and estimates of nitrogen and phosphorus loads, yields, and flow-weighted concentrations in base flow and runoff are provided. This report updates the work of Tortorelli (2008), which used water-quality and streamflow data from 2002 to 2006 and was a preliminary analysis of data collected for a multiyear monitoring program.

Nitrogen and phosphorus concentrations are compared among five stations in the Eucha-Spavinaw Basin and to concentrations measured at mostly undeveloped basins of the United States. Nitrogen and phosphorus loads are computed by using S-LOADEST, a program to compute mean constituent loads in rivers by using the rating-curve method (Dave Lorenz, U.S. Geological Survey, written commun., 2006). S-LOADEST, based on LOADEST (LOAD ESTimator, Runkel and others, 2004), uses instantaneous nutrient concentrations and daily mean streamflows to estimate mean annual and mean seasonal (spring, summer, autumn, and winter) nutrient loads and mean annual nutrient yields for the study period. This report provides information needed to advance knowledge of the regional hydrologic system and understanding of hydrologic processes and provides hydrologic data and results useful to multiple agencies for interstate agreements.

Study Area Description

The Eucha-Spavinaw Basin is a 415-square mile drainage basin divided between northeastern Oklahoma (70 percent), and northwestern Arkansas (30 percent) (fig. 1). Lake Eucha and Spavinaw Lake collect and store water from Spavinaw Creek and Beaty Creek, the main drainage channels for the basin, to supply the Tulsa metropolitan area and other local water users (Oklahoma Water Resources Board, 2002). The basin is in the southwestern part of the Ozark Plateaus physiographic province (Fenneman, 1938) and is underlain by the cherty limestone of the Springfield Plateau aquifer (Adamski and others, 1995). Soils are mostly classified as silty loam or gravelly silty loam (Storm and others, 2002).

The basin is dominated by pasture and hay and forested land, with interspersed minor amounts of urban land use (fig. 2). Spavinaw Creek Basin has more land covered by forest (39 percent) than Beaty Creek Basin (31 percent), and has less land covered by pasture and hay (54 percent) than Beaty Creek Basin (62 percent) (fig. 2). Nitrogen and phosphorus concentrations in Ozark streams typically are greater in streams draining agricultural lands than in streams draining forested lands (Petersen and others, 1998). Livestock production on pasture land is the primary form of agriculture in the basin; the basin is densely populated with poultry/beef cattle operations that use poultry litter as a fertilizer source for pastures (DeLaune and others, 2006, table 1). Litter application rates are greater in the Spavinaw Creek Basin than in Beaty Creek Basin (Storm and others, 2002, p. 25).

A municipal wastewater-treatment plant, operated by the city of Decatur, Arkansas, discharges an estimated 1.3 Mgal/d of wastewater effluent containing nitrogen and phosphorus to the Spavinaw Creek Basin according to data collected in 1999 (Haggard and others, 2001; Storm and others,

2002; DeLaune and others, 2006). This wastewater-treatment plant is referred to as the "Decatur wastewater-treatment plant" for this report. The Decatur wastewater-treatment plant has a wasteload allocation permit of 2.2 Mgal/d and a discharge limit of 1 milligram per liter (mg/L) total phosphorus and 10 mg/L ammonia as nitrogen (U.S. Environmental Protection Agency and Oklahoma Department of Environmental Quality, 2009). A smaller wastewater-treatment plant located in Beaty Creek Basin has a wasteload allocation permit of 0.56 Mgal/d, but nutrient contributions to Lake Eucha from that plant are considered substantially less because of the intermittent nature of the discharge (U.S. Environmental Protection Agency and Oklahoma Department of Environmental Quality, 2009). Streams receiving municipal wastewater from a treatment plant can have nitrogen and phosphorus concentrations substantially greater than concentrations in streams draining agricultural areas (Petersen and others, 1998).

Streamflow in the Eucha-Spavinaw Basin

Streamflow in the Eucha-Spavinaw Basin was highly varied from 2002 to 2009 and generally increased with basin drainage area (table 2, figs. 3–4). The maximum daily mean streamflow during the study period was in July 2004 for the three upstream Spavinaw Creek stations, March 2008 for the Colcord station, and January 2008 for the Beaty Creek station (table 2, fig. 3). The minimum daily mean streamflow during the study period was in August 2006 for the three upstream Spavinaw Creek stations; July 2006 at the Colcord station; and zero flow happened several times at the Beaty Creek station in September–October 2002, August 2003, October 2005, and July–October 2006 (table 2, fig. 3). Greatest monthly mean streamflows generally were from March through May and least monthly mean streamflows generally were from August through December at all stations (Blazs and others, 2003, 2004, 2005, 2006; U.S. Geological Survey, 2007, 2008b, 2009). Seasonal mean streamflows during the period 2002–2009 were greater for spring and winter than for summer and autumn (fig. 4). In this report, spring is March through May, summer is June through August, autumn is September through November, and winter is December through February.

Methods

This section describes the water-quality data-collection and analysis methods. These methods include streamflow separation into base flow and runoff, statistical tests used to compare groups of data, and methods used to estimate total nitrogen and phosphorus loads and yields. Flow-weighted nutrient concentrations for stations in undeveloped basins used to compare with the data collected in the Eucha-Spavinaw Basin also are presented.

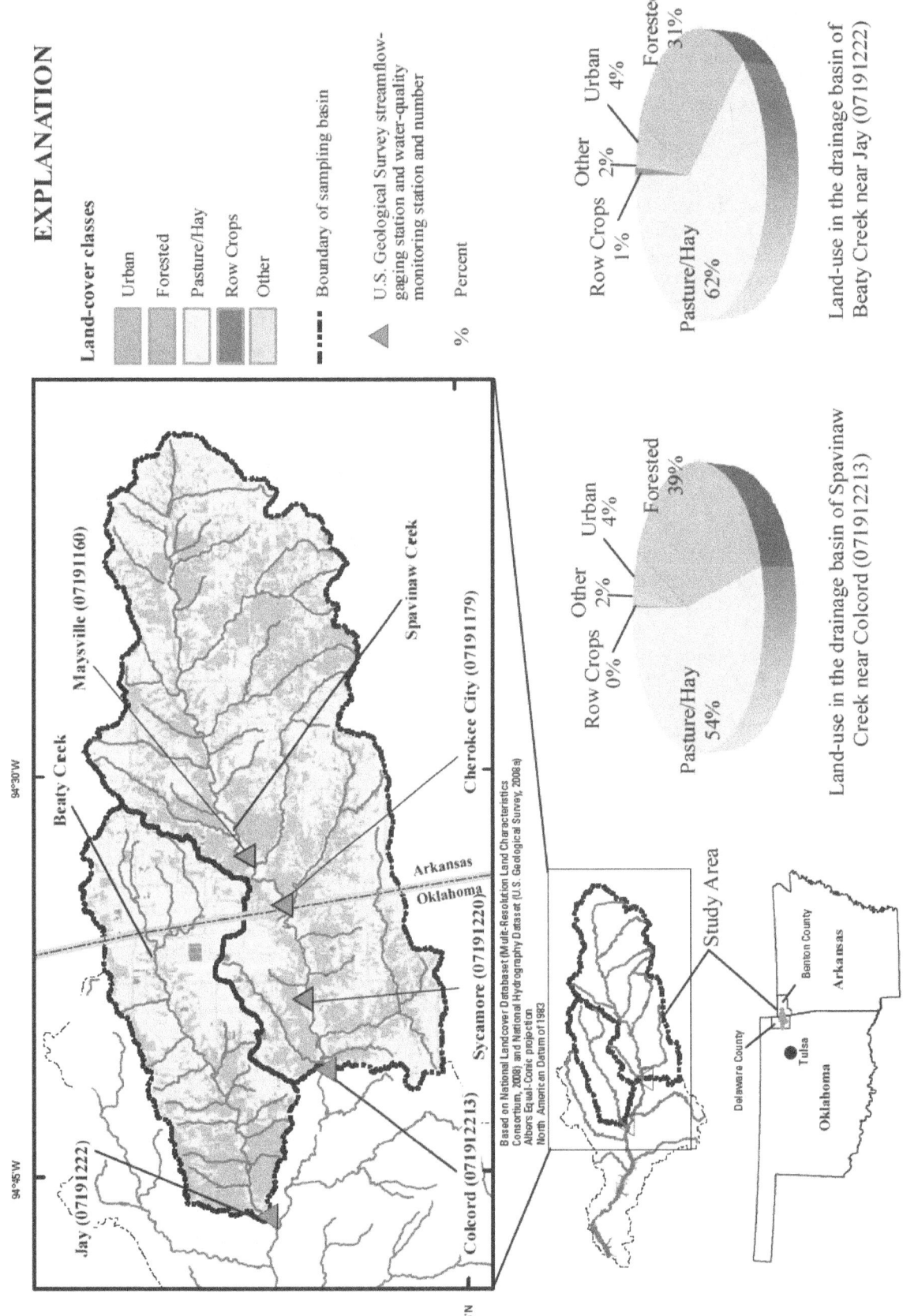

Figure 2.   Comparison of land use in the basins draining to Spavinaw Creek near Colcord, Oklahoma (07191213), and Beaty Creek near Jay, Oklahoma (07191222), in the Eucha-Spavinaw Basin, Arkansas and Oklahoma.

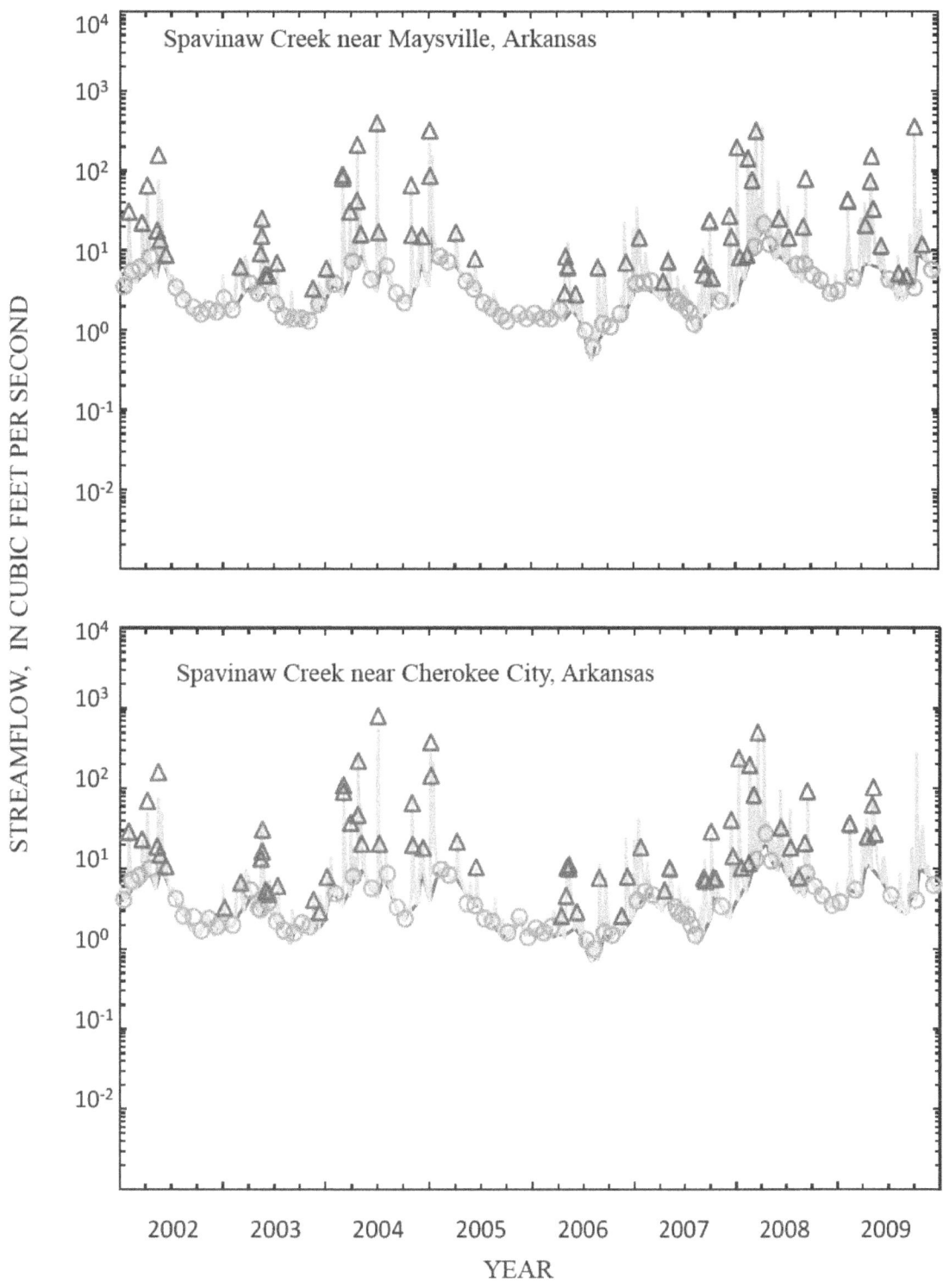

Figure 3. Streamflow divided into total flow and base flow, and base-flow and runoff water samples collected at water-quality stations in Eucha-Spavinaw Basin, Arkansas and Oklahoma, 2002–09.

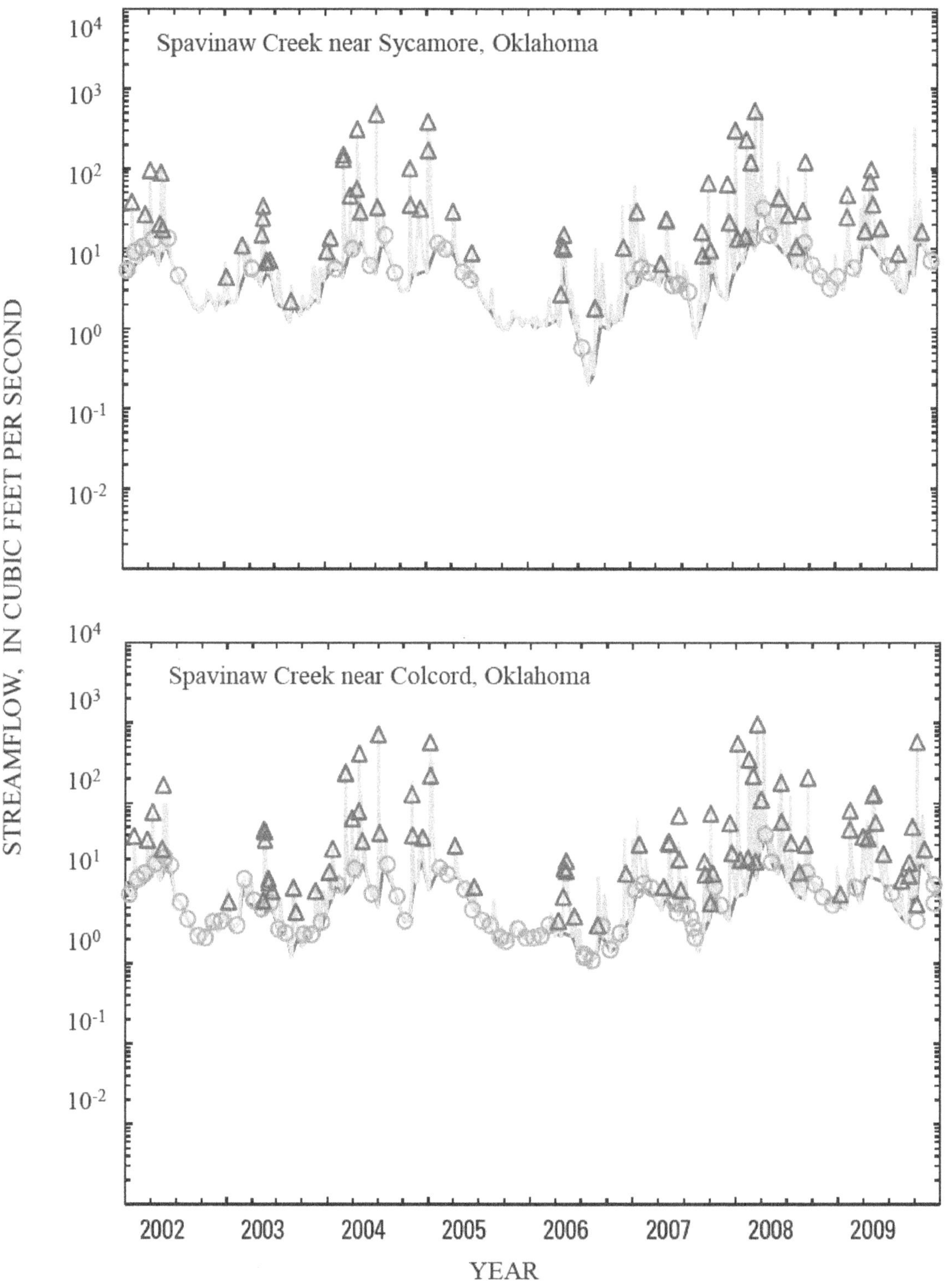

Figure 3.—Continued.

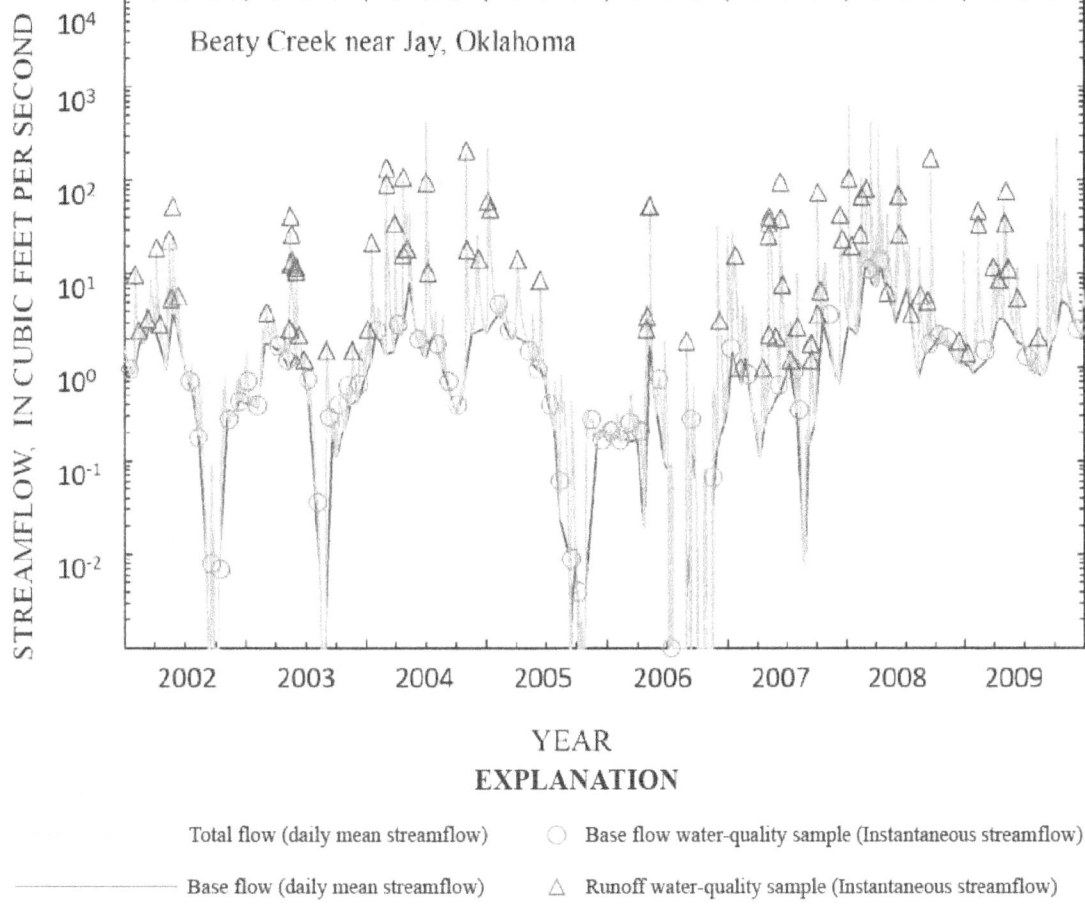

YEAR

EXPLANATION

———————— Total flow (daily mean streamflow)   ○ Base flow water-quality sample (Instantaneous streamflow)

———————— Base flow (daily mean streamflow)   △ Runoff water-quality sample (Instantaneous streamflow)

Figure 3.—Continued. .

Water-Quality Data Collection and Analysis

Streamflow-gaging stations were operated and stream-flows were measured according to methods described in Rantz and others (1982). Surface-water quality data used for load and yield estimation should represent a range of streamflow, from low to high, and be reasonably balanced among seasons (A.V. Vecchia, U.S. Geological Survey, written commun., 2005). Prior to July 2001, only scheduled, monthly water-quality samples were collected at these stations by staff from COT and included few runoff samples. Starting in July 2001 at the Cherokee City station, Colcord station, and Beaty Creek station and December 2001 at the Maysville station and Sycamore station, six rwater-quality samples were targeted to be collected annually during runoff at these stations by the USGS. Because of climate variability, more than six runoff samples were collected in some wet years and fewer than six runoff samples were collunoff ected in some dry years (fig. 3).

Representative water-quality samples were collected by USGS during high flow by using equal-width increment methods (Edwards and Glysson, 1999). USGS staff attempted to collect most runoff samples close to the storm peak, but some storm samples were collected before or after the storm peak. Samples collected by the COT, mostly during low flow at fixed monthly intervals, were collected at a single point near the midpoint of the stream. Fewer samples were collected from the Sycamore station than other stations because this station was located between the stations near Colcord, Oklahoma, and near Cherokee City, Arkansas. Samples for nitrogen and phosphorus constituents were not filtered in the field. Nitrogen and phosphorus concentrations represent both dissolved and particulate components.

The COT Water Quality Laboratory in Tulsa, Oklahoma, analyzed all water-quality samples by using methods described by the U.S. Environmental Protection Agency (U.S. Environmental Protection Agency, 1983, 1993). EPA method code

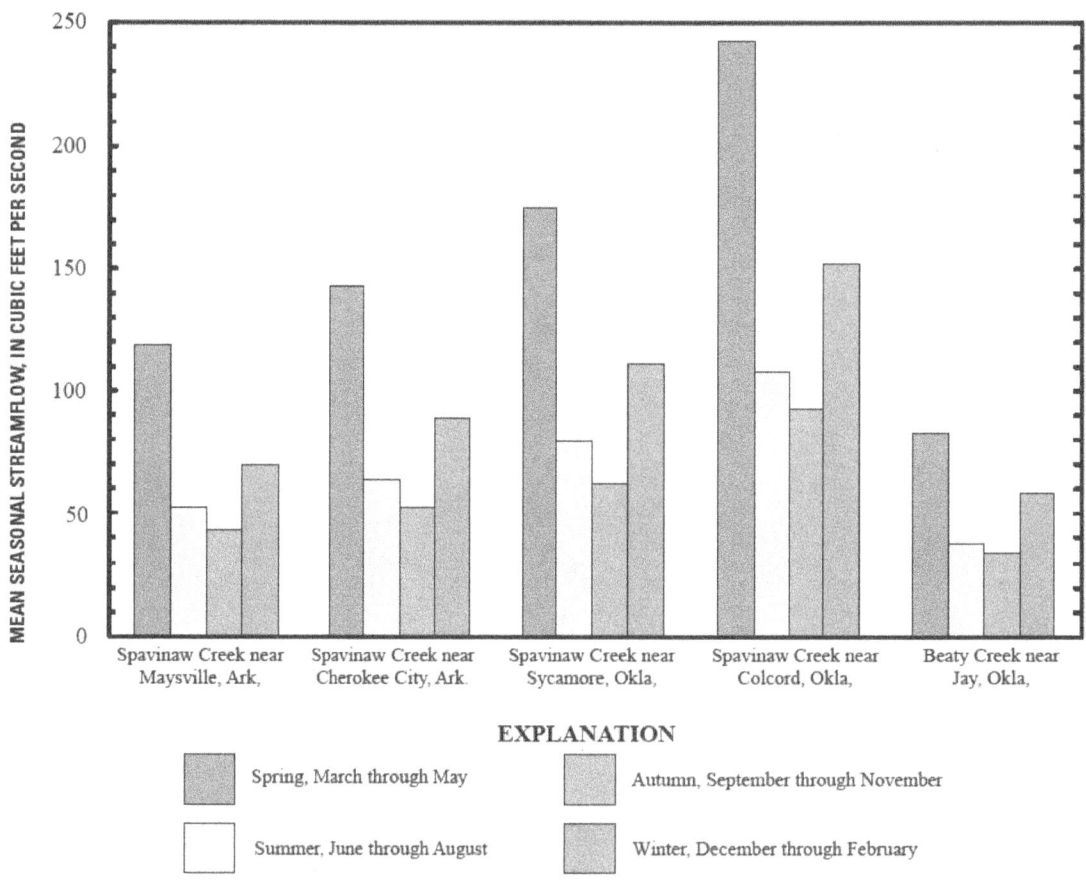

Figure 4.   Mean seasonal streamflow at five water-quality stations in the Eucha-Spavinaw Basin, Arkansas and Oklahoma, 2002–09.

Table 2.   Station information and streamflow statistics for surface-water and water-quality stations in the Eucha-Spavinaw Basin, Arkansas and Oklahoma, 2002–09.

[WY, water year (October 1 through September 30); mi², square mile; ft³/s, cubic foot per second]

Station name (number, fig. 1)	Period of record for station (WY)	Drainage area (mi²)	Annual mean streamflow for analysis period[1] (ft³/s)	Range of streamflow	
				Minimum streamflow (ft³/s and date)	Maximum streamflow (ft³/s and date)
Spavinaw Creek near Maysville, Ark. (07191160)	2002–present	88.2	71.0	4.2 (08/04/2006)	4,150 (07/03/2004)
Spavinaw Creek near Cherokee City, Ark. (07191179)	2002–present	104	86.9	7 (08/01/2006)	5,180 (07/03/2004)
Spavinaw Creek near Sycamore, Okla. (07191220)	1962–present	133	107.0	7.7 (08/18/2006)	6,300 (07/03/2004)
Spavinaw Creek near Colcord, Okla. (071912213)	2002–present	163	148.9	8.7 (07/29/2006)	8,720 (03/19/2008)
Beaty Creek near Jay, Okla. (07191222)	1998–present	59.2	53.1	0 at times (2002, 2003, 2005, 2006)	6,320 (01/8/2008)

[1] Analysis period for this report was January 1, 2002 to December 31, 2009.

351.2 was used to analyze for total Kjeldahl Nitrogen, EPA method code 353.2 was used to analyze for nitrate plus nitrite, and EPA method code 365.2 was used to analyze for total phosphorus (U.S. Environmental Protection Agency, 1983, 1993). Total nitrogen concentrations were calculated by adding total Kjeldahl Nitrogen (measure of ammonia plus organic nitrogen) and nitrite plus nitrate analyses. Total nitrogen and total phosphorus concentrations were reported if values were greater than the laboratory reporting level (LRL). The LRL is set to reduce false positive error and is equal to twice the yearly determined long-term method detection level (Childress and others, 1999).

Streamflow data and nitrogen and phosphorus concentration data collected from 2002 through 2009 were analyzed for this report. All streamflow and water-quality data in this report are available through the internet at *http://water.usgs.gov/ok/nwis*.

Quality assurance was achieved mainly through following a prescribed method of protocols and procedures as described in the National Field Manual (U.S. Geological Survey, 2006). Additionally, the collection and analysis of quality-control (QC) samples are mandated components of USGS water-quality field studies (U.S. Geological Survey, 2006) and compose an integral part of the overall quality assurance of the project. The goal of QC sampling is to identify, quantify, and document bias and variability in data that result from the collection, processing, shipping, and handling of samples. Field blanks and field sequential replicates were collected by the USGS at the rate of about 20 percent of the environmental samples. The COT collected QC samples at the rate of about 11 percent.

Two blank samples were collected from the Beaty Creek station in 2006 and one blank sample was collected from the Sycamore station in 2007. Total phosphorus concentrations were 0.011 and 0.006 mg/L in the two samples collected from the Beaty Creek station; whereas the total phosphorus concentration was nondetectable (<0.015 mg/L) in the blank sample collected at the Sycamore station. Total nitrogen constituents were nondetectable (<0.1 mg/L total Kjehldahl Nitrogen and <.047 mg/L nitrate plus nitrite) in the two blank samples collected at Beaty Creek. Total Kjehldahl Nitrogen was nondetectable (<0.1 mg/L) but the nitrate plus nitrite concentration was 0.22 mg/L for the blank sample collected at the Sycamore station. The results from the blank samples indicate that some contamination may have been as a result of sample collection or sample processing and some bias from potential contamination should be considered in evaluating the nutrient data in this report. Concentrations in field samples collected between 2002 and 2009 and used in this report ranged from 0.67 to 10.4 mg/L for total nitrogen and 0.02 to 1.60 mg/L for total phosphorus. Sequential replicate analyses were conducted for 78 samples: 13 replicate samples were collected from the Maysville Station, 10 replicate samples were collected from the Cherokee City station, 10 replicate samples were collected from the Sycamore station, 2 replicate samples were collected from the Colcord station, and 43 replicate samples were collected from the Beaty Creek station,. The relative percentage difference between sequential replicate analyses for nitrate plus nitrite, the main component of total nitrogen, was less than 1 percent. The relative percentage difference between sequential replicate total phosphorus analyses was 3 percent.

Streamflow Separation

Streamflow was separated into base-flow and runoff components by using a hydrograph separation program, Base-Flow Index (Institute of Hydrology, 1980a, 1980b; Wahl and Wahl, 1995) (fig. 3). Base flow is considered the runoff sustained after the end of storm runoff or fair-weather flow of the stream. Base flow is largely composed of ground-water seepage (Langbein and Iseri, 1960). Base-flow and runoff components were separated because base-flow concentrations are more indicative of point sources, and runoff concentrations are more indicative of nonpoint sources. The minimum daily mean flow was identified in consecutive 5-day increments, and minimums less than 90 percent of adjacent minimums were defined as turning points (Wahl and Wahl, 1995). The Base-Flow Index program estimated the base-flow hydrograph by drawing straight lines through successive turning points. Runoff components were calculated as the difference between total streamflow and base-flow components.

The mean fraction of annual total flow that was runoff, computed by using streamflow data for the period 2002–2009, ranged from 44 to 50 percent at stations on Spavinaw Creek and 69 percent at the Beaty Creek station (table 3). The lesser runoff percentage at Spavinaw Creek may indicate a greater proportion of groundwater inputs in the Spavinaw Creek Basin than in the Beaty Creek Basin.

Each day of the study period was designated to be base flow or runoff by using results from the base-flow index program. Base-flow days in this report were defined as days during which base flow contributed greater than or equal to

Table 3. Mean base-flow index for surface-water and water-quality stations in the Eucha-Spavinaw Basin, Arkansas and Oklahoma, 2002–09.

Station name (number)	Mean base-flow index (percent)[1]	Mean percent runoff
Spavinaw Creek near Maysville, Ark. (07191160)	56	44
Spavinaw Creek near Cherokee City, Ark. (07191179)	54	46
Spavinaw Creek near Sycamore, Okla. (07191220)	50	50
Spavinaw Creek near Colcord, Okla. (071912213)	52	48
Beaty Creek near Jay, Okla. (07191222)	31	69

[1] The mean ratio of base flow to total flow, computed using the Base-Flow Index computer program (Institute of Hydrology, 1980a,1980b; Wahl and Wahl, 1995).

70 percent of total flow; runoff days were defined as days during which runoff contributed greater than 30 percent of total flow (Tortorelli and Pickup, 2006; Tortorelli, 2006).

Statistical Tests

The Mann-Whitney rank-sum test (Helsel and Hirsch, 1992), used to compare the median and distribution of two independent groups of data, was used to determine the statistical significance of differences between base-flow and runoff nitrogen concentrations and base-flow and runoff phosphorus concentrations in samples collected at each station in the study period. Mann-Whitney rank-sum tests were performed to compare differences between base-flow and runoff nutrient concentrations in samples collected during the entire period and between base-flow and runoff nutrient concentrations in samples collected during different seasons (spring, summer, autumn, and winter). The Mann-Whitney test was not performed for any given season if less than 10 base-flow or runoff samples were available for comparison.

The Kruskal-Wallis test (Helsel and Hirsch, 1992), used to compare multiple datasets at one time, was used to determine the statistical significance of differences in nitrogen and phosphorus concentrations among seasons in base-flow and runoff data groups for each station. The Kruskal-Wallis test also was used to determine the statistical significance of differences in nitrogen and phosphorus concentrations among stations in the Eucha-Spavinaw Basin in base-flow and runoff data groups in samples collected during the entire period.

The Mann-Whitney and Kruskal-Wallis statistical tests were selected because the tests do not require normally distributed data. The null hypothesis of the tests is no differences in the median and distribution of concentrations among the datasets being compared. The null hypothesis was rejected and concentrations were described as being significantly different if the two-sided p-value of the test was less than or equal to 0.05 (Helsel and Hirsch, 1992). If the null hypothesis of the Kruskal-Wallis test was rejected and the concentrations were described as being significantly different, the multiple-stage Kruskal-Wallis test was applied to determine which seasons were different or which stations were different and which were not (Helsel and Hirsch, 1992).

Load and Yield Estimation

Linear regression was used to evaluate relations between nitrogen and phosphorus loads (dependent variables) and streamflow and time (independent variables). Daily nitrogen and phosphorus loads could not be calculated directly because water-quality data were collected intermittently. Regression methods allow estimation of daily water-quality constituent loads by using continuous streamflow records. Regression methods require daily mean streamflow data and discrete water-quality samples collected during several years. Sample dates, times, streamflows, and nitrogen and phosphorus concentrations for discrete water-quality samples used in this analysis are provided in appendixes 1–5 and are available through the internet at *http://water.usgs.gov/ok/nwis*.

Load is the amount of a constituent transported past a selected point in a stream in a given amount of time. Constituent load (L) is the product of streamflow (Q) and the constituent concentration in the water (C) multiplied by a conversion factor to convert cubic feet per second (ft³/s) and milligrams per liter (mg/L) to pounds per day (lb/d). The S-LOADEST program (Dave Lorenz, U.S. Geological Survey, written commun., 2006) was used to estimate constituent loads in the Eucha-Spavinaw Basin by the rating-curve method (Cohn and others, 1989; Crawford, 1991). S-LOADEST is based on LOADEST (Runkel and others, 2004) and is incorporated in the computer program Spotfire S-Plus (TIBCO Software Incorporated, 2008) to facilitate graphical analysis and tabular results. S-LOADEST estimates rating-curve parameters and mean daily loads by using maximum likelihood regression methods (Dempster and others, 1977; Wolynetz, 1979; Cohn, 1988; and Cohn and others, 1992). S-LOADEST contains nine predefined rating-curve models that can test the relation between constituent load and streamflow. The model used for this report (equation 1) includes time variables and seasonality variables to simulate the relation between the natural logarithms of L, Q, and Q^2 by using a derivation of the following equation:

$$\ln(L) = b_o + b_1 \ln Q + b_2 \ln Q^2 + b_3 T + b_4 T^2 + b_5 \sin SS + b_6 \cos SS \tag{1}$$

where

ln	is natural logarithm
L	is constituent load, in pounds per day;
b_0	is regression constant, dimensionless;
$b_1, b_2, b_3, b_4, b_5, b_6$	are regression coefficients, dimensionless;
Q	is daily mean streamflow, in cubic feet per second;
T	is dectime, time parameter in decimal years;
sin	is sine;
SS	is seasonality parameter (2πdectime); and
cos	is cosine.

S-LOADEST allows users to select the "best" model to estimate constituent load given a various combination of streamflow, time, and seasonal coefficients, by using one or all the variables from equation (1). S-LOADEST computes the Akaike Information Content (AIC) from each possible model, and the model with the lowest AIC is selected as the "best" model (Runkel and others, 2004) that most closely fits the data with a minimum number of independent variables (Akaike, 1974).

Modeling scenarios in equation 1 will have multicollinearity present between the streamflow and time terms (Q and T, respectively) because the quadratic terms are included in the regression model. Multicollinearty arises when one of the independent variables is related to one or more of the other independent variables (Helsel and Hirsch, 1992). The presence of collinear independent variables is undesirable because it confounds interpretation of model coefficients and tests of the significance (Runkel and others, 2004; p. 13). To avoid multi-collinearity, S-LOADEST computes the center of the calibration data (Cohn and others, 1992) with the following equation:

$$\hat{C} = \overline{C} + \frac{\sum\limits_{k=1}^{N}\left(C - \overline{C}\right)^3}{2\sum\limits_{k=1}^{N}\left(C - \overline{C}\right)^2} \qquad (2)$$

Where,

$\hat{C}$ is the centering constant for the S-LOADEST calibration dataset,

N is the number of observations in S-LOADEST calibration data set and is an integer that defines the upper bound of summation,

k is the first integer of the lower bound of summatio

$\overline{C}$ is the mean of the data, and

C is the quantity to be centered (decimal time or the natural logarithm of daily mean streamflow).

Within S-LOADEST, $\hat{C}$ is subtracted from each C in the calibration dataset, and the resulting "centered" values are used to develop the linear model. As a result, the linear and quadratic terms are orthogonal and no longer collinear.

Separate linear regression models were developed in S-LOADEST for the estimation of nitrogen and phosphorus loads for the period 2002–09 at each station. The regression models developed by S-LOADEST are listed in tables 4 and 5. The centering constants for each variable are included for each regression model.

The "best" model indicated in S-LOADEST was different for each nutrient and station. One general model (based on equation 1) was selected for all stations for each nutrient: (1) to use a consistent general model to estimate daily loads at all stations in the basin for each nutrient, and (2) because an analysis of the "best" models compared with this general model indicated a very small improvement in reduction in variance for each estimate. Each final model selected to estimate daily nitrogen and phosphorus load included the least number of independent variables that contained all the independent variables selected for any of the "best" models for each constituent and station (tables 4 and 5). The general equation selected to estimate daily nitrogen load for all stations was the same as equation 1. The general equation selected to estimate daily phosphorus load for each station was similar to equation 1, but did not include a quadratic term for time (T^2) because the quadratic form of this variable was not a statistically significant estimator of phosphorus load at the 95 percent confidence limit in any of the regression equations.

Only one model was developed for each nutrient at all stations for the period 2002–09 in this report. In previous reports, 3-year periods were used to average annual climate variation and to emulate a 3-year moving average (Tortorelli, 2006, 2008). Different model coefficients for each 3-year period (2002–04, 2003–05, and 2004–06) were used in previous reports to allow the slope between L and Q to vary

Table 4. Regression models for estimating total nitrogen loads at water-quality stations in the Eucha-Spavinaw Basin, Arkansas and Oklahoma, developed by using data collected during 2002–09.

[no., number; obs., observations; ln, natural logarithm; L, daily load in pound per day; Q, mean daily streamflow in cubic foot per second; T, decimal time, time parameter in decimal years; sin, sine; cos, cosine; SS, seasonality parameter; R^2, coefficient of determination]

Station name (number)	No. of obs.	Total nitrogen load regression model[1]	Estimated residual variance[2]	R^2 (percent)
Spavinaw Creek near Maysville, Ark. (07191160)	139	ln(L) = 8.09 + 1.13*(lnQ-4.93) - 0.018*(lnQ-4.93)² - 0.005*(T-2005.92) + 0.002*(T-2005.92)² - 0.013*sin SS + 0.14*cos SS	0.048	98.3
Spavinaw Creek near Cherokee City, Ark. (07191179)	140	ln(L) = 8.44 + 1.08*(lnQ-5.18) - 0.015*(lnQ-5.18)² + 0.002*(T-2005.92) - 0.002*(T-2005.92)² + 0.002*sin SS + 0.176*cos SS	.026	99.0
Spavinaw Creek near Sycamore, Okla. (07191220)	102	ln(L) = 8.78 + 1.07*(lnQ-5.41) + 0.003*(lnQ-5.41)² - 0.001*(T-2005.92) - 0.003*(T-2005.92)² + 0.012*sin SS + .169*cos SS	.021	99.1
Spavinaw Creek near Colcord, Okla. (071912213)	152	ln(L) = 8.66 + 1.10*(lnQ-5.50) - 0.010*(lnQ-5.50)² - 0.006*(T-2005.97) - 0.001*(T-2005.97)² + 0.025*sin SS + 0.176*cos SS	.029	99
Beaty Creek near Jay, Okla. (07191222)	146	ln(L) = 5.51 + 1.14*(lnQ-2.80) - 0.001*(lnQ-2.80)² + 0.014*(T-2005.99) + 0.013*(T-2005.99)² + 0.124*sin SS - 0.124*cos SS	.076	98.9

[1] The seasonality parameter (SS) is computed as 2*π*dectime.

[2] Estimated residual variance is the variance corrected for the number of observations and number of parameters in the regression model.

Table 5. Regression models for estimating total phosphorus loads at water-quality stations in the Eucha-Spavinaw Basin, Arkansas and Oklahoma, developed by using data collected during 2002–09.

[no., number; obs., observations; ln, natural logarithm; L, daily load in pound per day; Q, mean daily streamflow in cubic foot per second; T, decimal time, time parameter in decimal years; sin, sine; cos, cosine; SS, seasonality parameter; R^2, coefficient of determination]

Station name (number)	No. of obs.	Total phosphorus load regression model[1]	Estimated residual variance[2]	R^2 (per-cent)
Spavinaw Creek near Maysville, Ark. (07191160)	133	$\ln(L) = 3.63 + 1.54*(\ln Q-4.93) + 0.159*(\ln Q-4.93)^2 + 0.023*(T-2005.93)$ $- 0.089*\sin SS - 0.135*\cos SS$	0.200	96.3
Spavinaw Creek near Chero-kee City, Ark. (07191179)	136	$\ln(L) = 4.80 + 1.22*(\ln Q-5.18) + 0.146*(\ln Q-5.18)^2 - 0.125*(T-2005.93)$ $- 0.125*\sin SS + 0.005*\cos SS$	.126	96.0
Spavinaw Creek near Syca-more, Okla. (07191220)	100	$\ln(L) = 4.91 + 1.30*(\ln Q-5.41) + 0..123*(\ln Q-5.41)^2 - 0.084*(T-2005.92)$ $- 0.014*\sin SS - 0.044*\cos SS$	.101	97.1
Spavinaw Creek near Colcord, Okla. (071912213)	148	$\ln(L) = 5.06 + 1.37*(\ln Q-5.50) + 0.093*(\ln Q-5.50)^2 - 0.061*(T-2005.97)$ $- 0.062*\sin SS - 0.081*\cos SS$	.169	96.0
Beaty Creek near Jay, Okla. (07191222)	144	$\ln(L) = 1.31 + 1.30*\ln(Q-2.80) + 0.059*\ln(Q-2.80)^2 + 0.018*(T-2005.99)$ $- 0.178*\sin SS - 0.075*\cos SS$	.149	98.4

[1] The seasonality parameter (SS) is computed as $2*\pi*$dectime.

[2] Estimated residual variance is the variance corrected for the number of observations and number of parameters in the regression model.

with time instead of having one slope for the 5-year period, 2002–06, to improve model fit. However, the variability of the slope between L and Q with time is accounted for in one model by including time (T) as a parameter in the regression model. The use of one equation facilitates comparison of resulting models for each station for the entire sampling period and is a more efficient means of computing total constituent load because only one estimate of annual load is generated (David K. Mueller, U.S. Geological Survey, oral and written commun., April 2009). Annual and seasonal load estimates presented in this report may differ slightly from estimates presented in Tortorelli (2008) because an updated load model was used.

The use of one equation also is helpful for evaluation of changes in the slope between L and Q with time (T) for the entire sampling period. A statistically significant time variable (T) that is positive or negative may signify a trend in flow-adjusted constituent concentrations during the sampling period that is upward or downward, respectively (Helsel and Hirsch, 1992, p. 337–371). Further evaluation of the time variable may be used to assess the statistical significance and magnitude of trends in constituent concentration over time. Documentation of the significance and magnitude of trends in nitrogen and phosphorus concentrations over time was beyond the scope of this report.

For consistency with previous publications (Tortorelli, 2006, 2008), S-LOADEST was used to estimate daily con-stituent load, which was used to compute annual loads. All annual loads are computed by calendar year (January 1 to December 31). The daily load estimate from the S-LOADEST model is considered a daily mean load, and instantaneous

loads were not estimated. A limitation of this approach is the assumption that daily mean load is not substantially different than maximum or minimum instantaneous load. A potential bias of this approach is that total daily load may be over or underestimated, depending on the flow condition (Christensen and others, 2008; Tortorelli, 2008). Such bias may occur during extremely flashy runoff because peak instantaneous streamflow is substantially greater than daily mean stream-flow resulting in a total daily load that is greater than daily mean load. Therefore, the S-LOADEST methods used in this approach may underestimate total constituent load at a daily time scale. This bias may affect the computation of annual load from daily load estimates during years in which substan-tial runoff events are frequent.

Data from most stations generally fit the model better for nitrogen than for phosphorus (tables 4 and 5). Data from the Beaty Creek station fit the model for phosphorus better than data from the Spavinaw stations, as indicated by a higher coefficient of determination (R^2) for the Beaty Creek load model (table 5). The R^2 of a model is the square of sample cor-relation coefficient that is a measure of differences in observed data and data estimated from the model (Helsel and Hirsch, 1992) and ranges from 0 to 1. An R^2 of 1 indicates no differ-ence between observed and estimated data (Helsel and Hirsch, 1992). Nitrogen S-LOADEST equation coefficients for Q and T terms were similar to the equation coefficients reported in Tortorelli (2008) for all three 3-year moving periods. Phos-phorus S-LOADEST equation coefficients for Q terms were similar to the equation coefficients reported in Tortorelli (2008), but the T terms were not comparable because the S-LOADEST equation from this report did not include a squared T term; whereas, this term was included in the phosphorus S-LOADEST equations reported previously.

Estimated mean annual nitrogen and phosphorus loads and estimates of the standard deviations of the mean loads were calculated by S-LOADEST by using all base-flow and runoff data. The daily load values generated by S-LOADEST were separated into base-flow and runoff sample sets according to the number of base-flow days and the number of runoff days for the entire sampling period. Estimated mean annual base-flow loads were calculated as the mean of the base-flow day sample set. Estimated mean annual runoff loads were calculated as the mean of the runoff day sample set. Estimated seasonal base-flow and runoff loads were calculated in the same way on the basis of the number of base-flow and runoff days in each season.

Nitrogen and phosphorus yields for the study period at each station were calculated by dividing mean annual nitrogen and phosphorus loads by drainage area (table 2). Flow-weighted concentrations for the study period at each station were calculated by dividing mean annual nitrogen and phosphorus loads by mean annual streamflow and multiplying by a conversion factor to adjust the units.

Nutrient Concentrations in Undeveloped Basins

Flow-weighted nitrogen and phosphorus concentrations were compared among stations in the Eucha-Spavinaw Basin. Flow-weighted concentrations also were compared with the median and 75th percentile of flow-weighted total nitrogen and phosphorus concentrations of mostly undeveloped basins. These comparisons were from streams draining 85 mostly undeveloped basins from across the United States. These streams were selected from three programs of the USGS—the Hydrologic Benchmark Network (Cobb and Biesecker, 1971; Mast and Turk, 1999), the National Water-Quality Assessment program (Gilliom and others, 1995, 2001), and the USGS National Research Program (Clark and others, 2000).

The USGS National Research Program provided research data for the assessment of flow-weighted total nitrogen and phosphorus concentrations in Clark and others (2000) from 20 USGS research basins nationwide. These small basins ranged in size from about 0.04 to 8.5 square miles and were predominately in the Appalachian and Rocky Mountains (Clark and others, 2000).

Nutrient Concentrations, Loads, and Yields in the Eucha-Spavinaw Basin

Nitrogen and phosphorus in the Eucha-Spavinaw Basin are described in terms of mean concentrations, loads, and yields from base-flow and runoff samples, and in terms of mean flow-weighted concentrations. All annual and seasonal loads, yields, and flow-weighted concentrations are estimated mean values that were calculated by S-LOADEST. All total nitrogen values are referred to as nitrogen and total phosphorus values are referred to as phosphorus in the remainder of this report.

Concentrations

The summary statistics of nitrogen and phosphorus concentrations in water samples for the entire analysis period by season, divided into base-flow and runoff samples, are presented in tables 6 and 7. Results from the Mann-Whitney test of constituent concentrations in base-flow and runoff samples are presented in table 8. Boxplots showing comparisons of concentrations among stations for base-flow and runoff samples as a result of the Kruskal-Wallis test are shown in figure 5. Boxplots showing comparisons of concentrations among seasons for base flow and runoff samples as a result of the Kruskal-Wallis test are presented in figures 6 and 7. Base flow or runoff distributions with the same letter are not significantly different (p less than or equal 0.05) as a result of the Kruskal-Wallis test on distributions for each station (figs. 5–7). Two letters indicate the distribution was not different from more than one data set (fig. 5). Graphs showing the nutrient concentrations in base-flow and runoff samples are presented in figures 8 and 9.

The Mann-Whitney test was not performed to test statistical differences in constituent concentrations from base-flow and runoff samples for the summer, autumn, and winter seasons for nitrogen and the autumn and winter seasons for phosphorus for the Sycamore station because less than 10 base-flow samples were collected for each constituent during these seasons (tables 6 and 7). The Kruskal-Wallis test also was not performed for testing statistical differences among seasonal concentrations in samples collected at this station because less than 10 samples were collected during the seasons previously listed.

Nitrogen

Nitrogen concentrations were significantly different ($p \leq 0.05$) between runoff samples and base-flow samples collected during the entire period from most stations except for samples collected at the Sycamore station (table 8). Boxplots indicate that nitrogen concentrations were greater in runoff samples than in base-flow samples (fig. 5–6) where concentrations were significantly different as a result of the Mann-Whitney test (table 8). Significant differences in nitrogen concentrations in base-flow and runoff samples were variable by season and station. Nitrogen concentrations were significantly greater in runoff samples than in base-flow samples collected during the summer, autumn, and winter seasons from the Maysville station and the Beaty Creek station. Nitrogen concentrations were significantly greater in

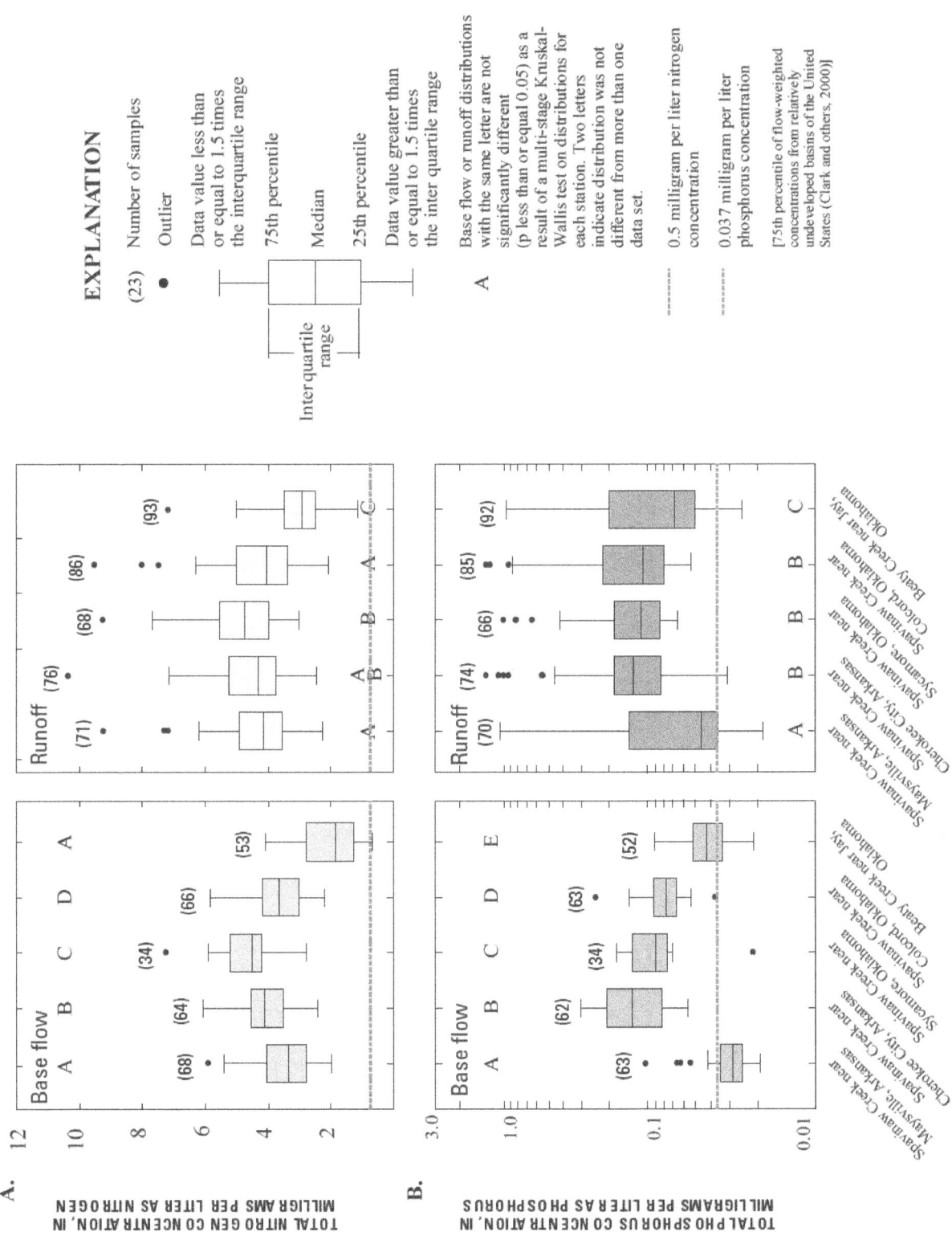

Figure 5. Distribution of (A) total nitrogen and (B) total phosphorus concentrations in water samples collected at water-quality stations in the Eucha-Spavinaw Basin, Arkansas and Oklahoma, 2002–09.

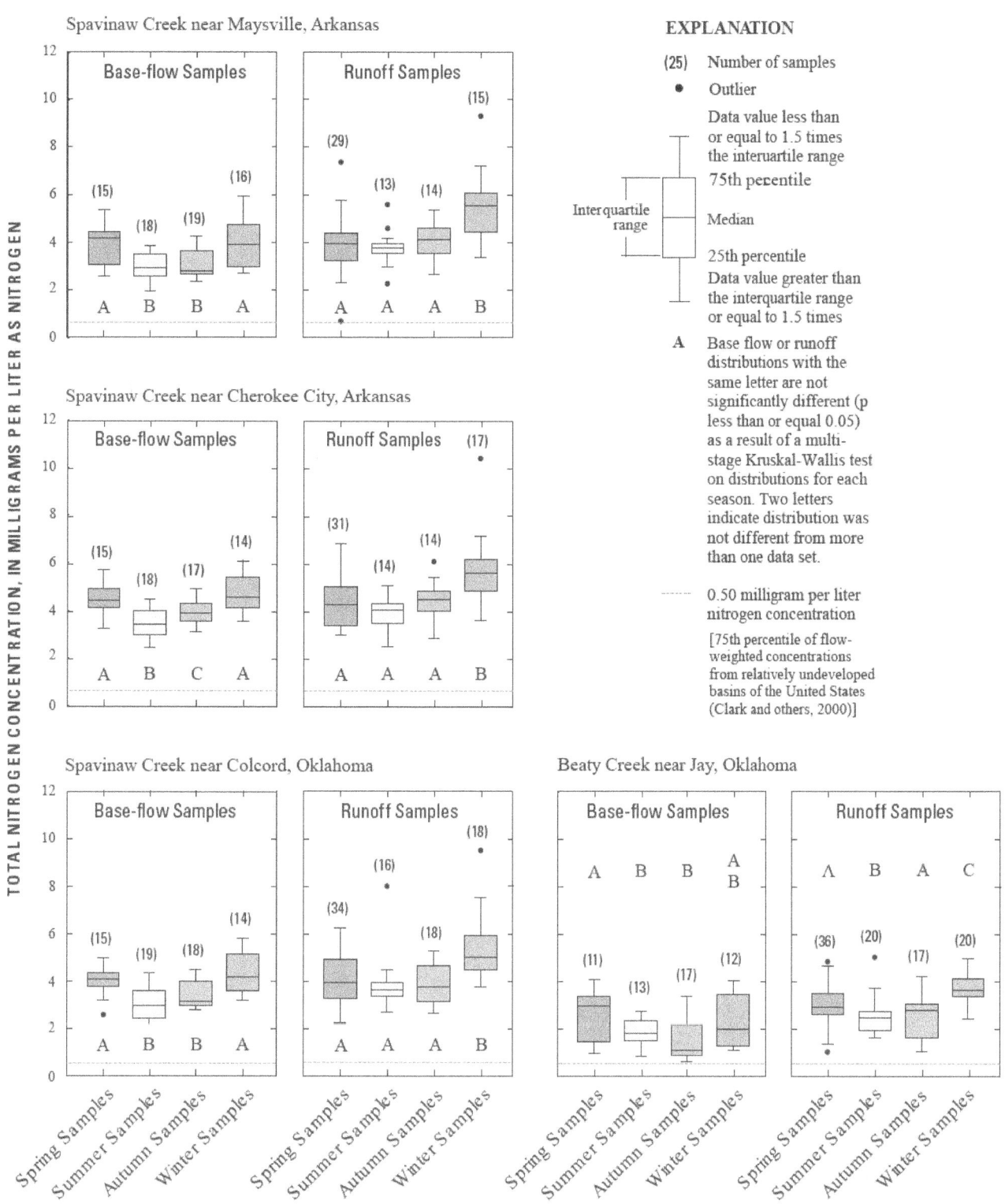

Figure 6. Distributions of seasonal total nitrogen concentrations in water samples collected at water-quality stations in the Eucha-Spavinaw Basin, Arkansas and Oklahoma, 2002–09.

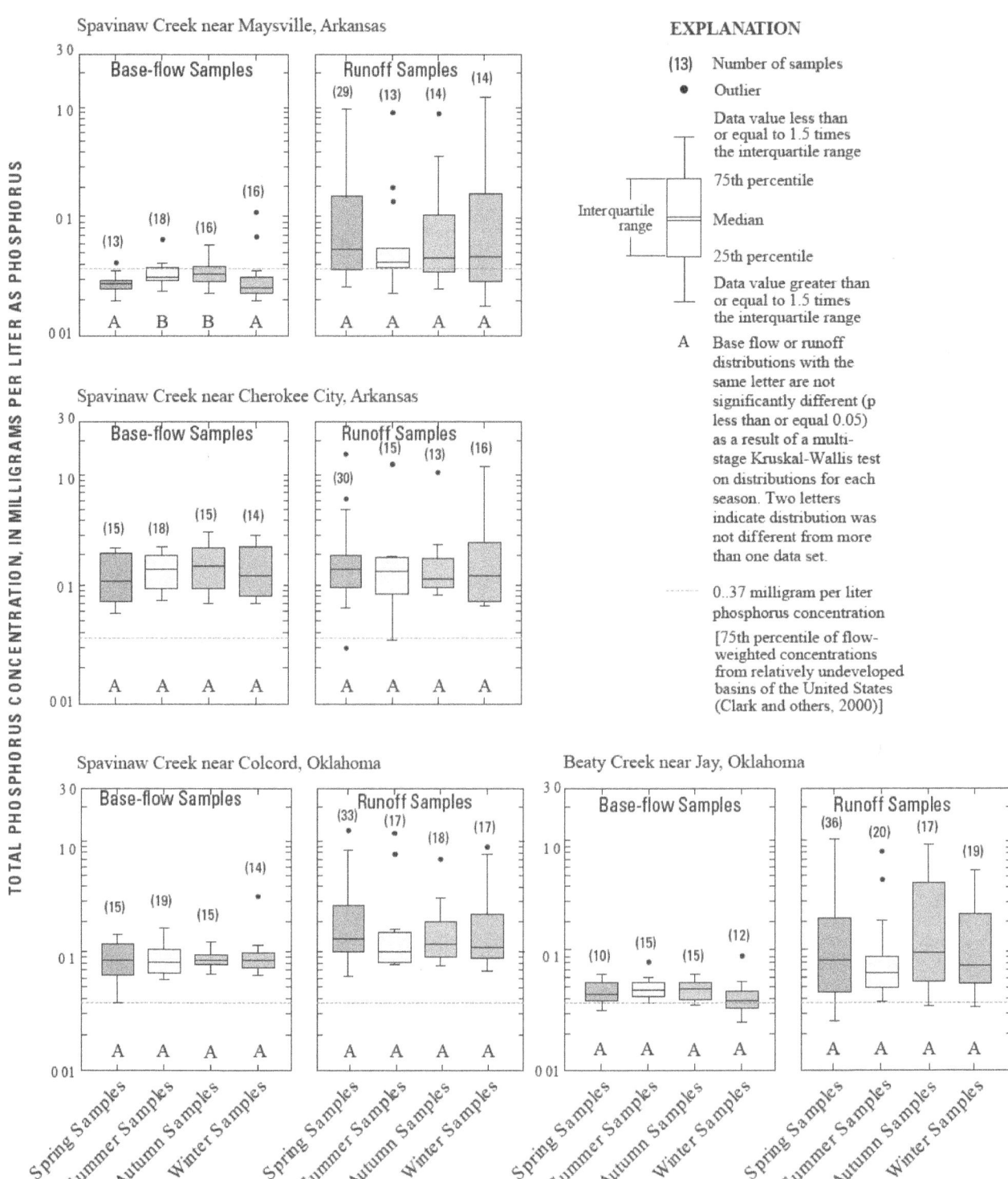

Figure 7. Distributions of seasonal total phosphorus concentrations in water samples collected at water-quality stations in the Eucha-Spavinaw Basin, Arkansas and Oklahoma, 2002–09.

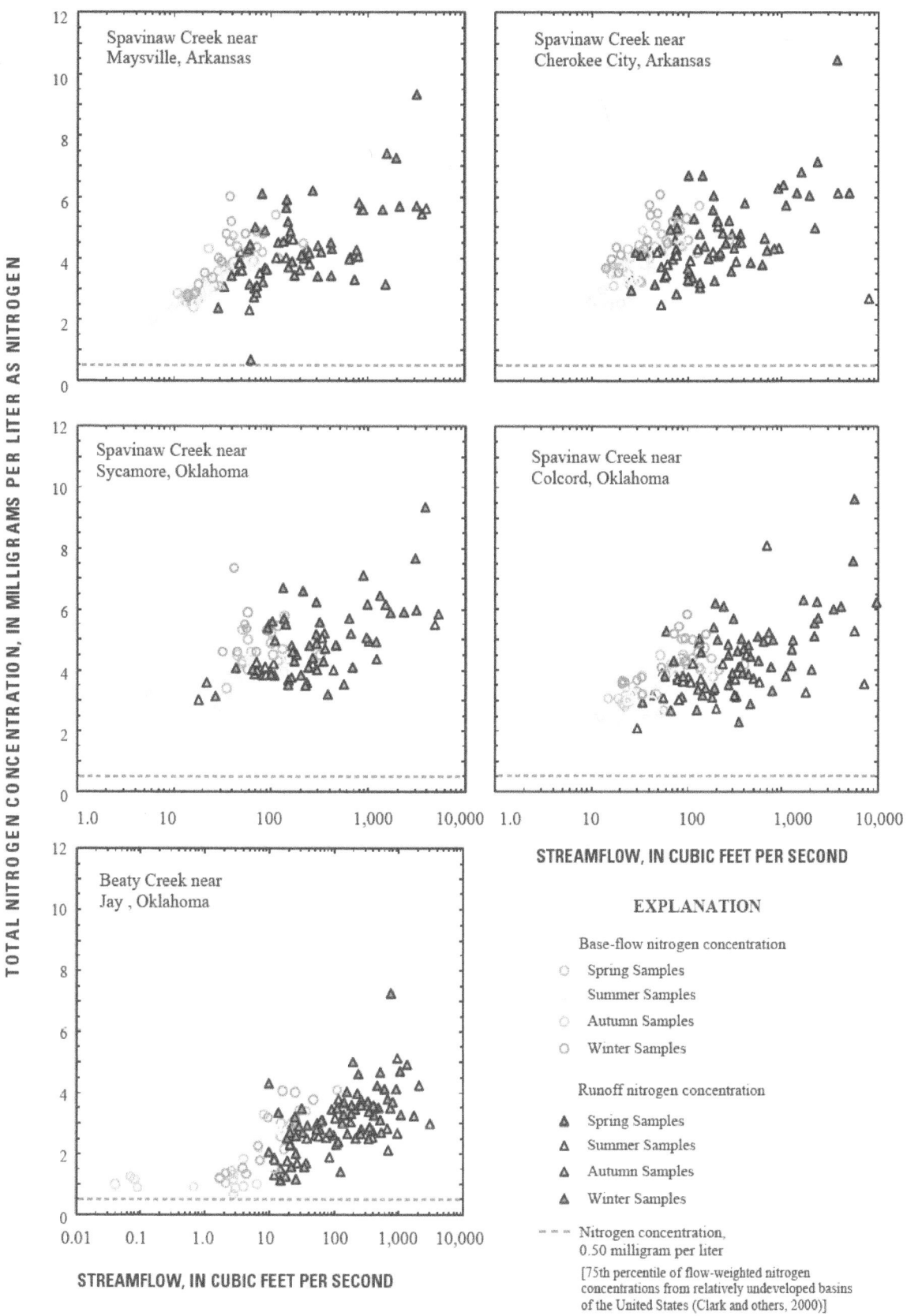

Figure 8. Total nitrogen concentrations in base-flow and runoff water samples collected at water-quality stations in the Eucha-Spavinaw Basin, Arkansas and Oklahoma, 2002–09.

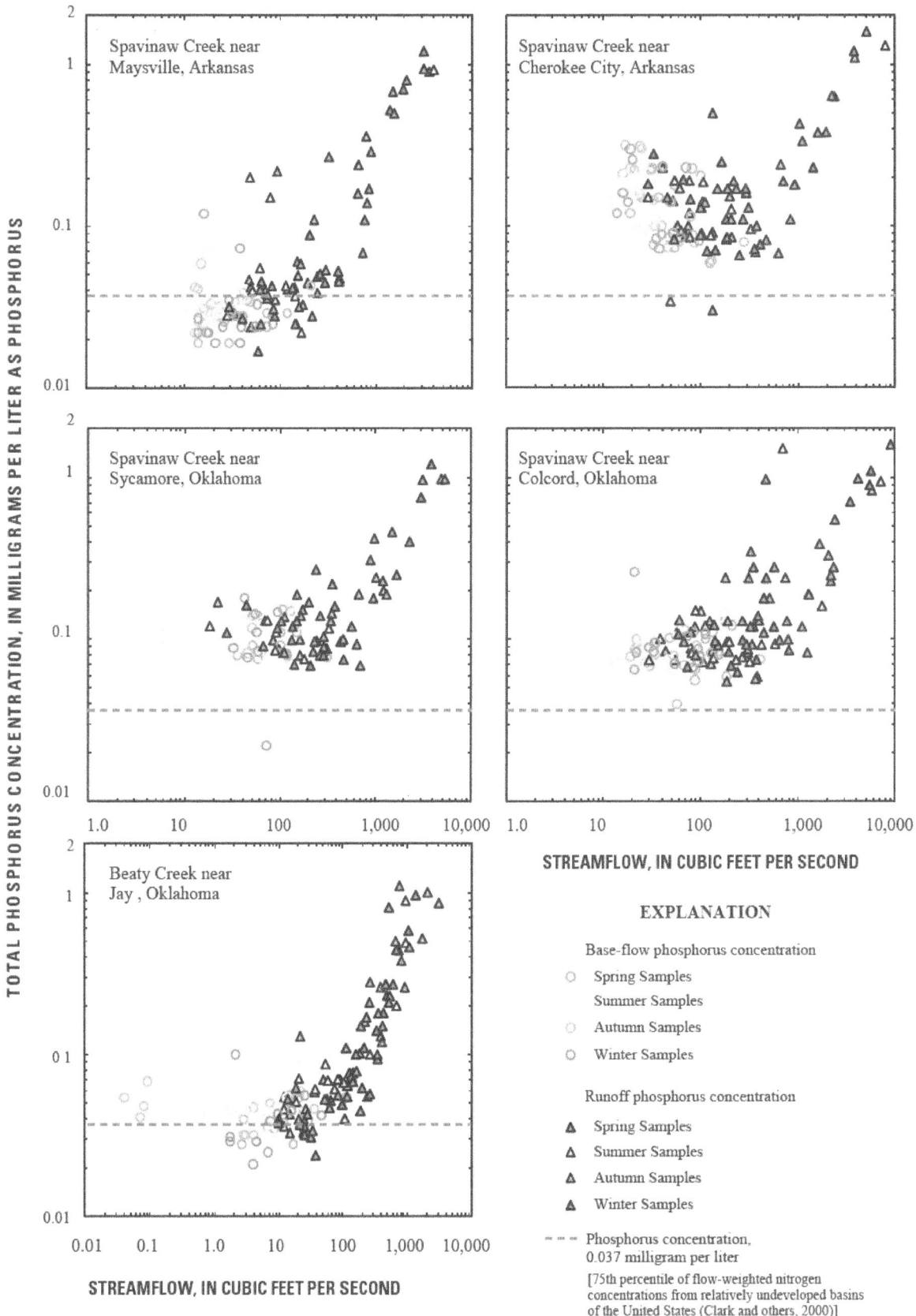

Figure 9.   Total phosphorus concentrations in base-flow and runoff water samples collected at water-quality stations in the Eucha-Spavinaw Basin, Arkansas and Oklahoma, 2002–09.

Table 6. Summary statistics of total nitrogen concentrations in base-flow and runoff water samples collected at water-quality stations in the Eucha-Spavinaw Basin, Arkansas and Oklahoma, 2002–09.

[Obs, number of observations; mg/L, milligram per liter; N, nitrogen]

Station name (number)	Time period	Base-flow concentrations					Runoff concentrations				
		Obs	Mini-mum	Median	Mean	Maxi-mum	Obs	Mini-mum	Median	Mean	Maxi-mum
			(mg/L as N)					(mg/L as N)			
Spavinaw Creek near Maysville, Ark. (07191160)	All Seasons	68	1.98	3.36	3.50	6.00	71	0.69	4.16	4.32	9.34
	Spring	15	2.60	4.20	3.98	5.40	29	.69	3.97	4.01	7.40
	Summer	18	1.98	2.98	3.07	3.91	13	2.29	3.82	3.84	5.61
	Autumn	19	2.39	2.85	3.12	4.30	14	2.71	4.18	4.10	5.43
	Winter	16	2.73	3.95	3.97	6.00	15	3.40	5.57	5.54	9.34
Spavinaw Creek near Cherokee City, Ark. (07191179)	All Seasons	64	2.45	4.12	4.08	6.08	76	2.48	4.31	4.59	10.4
	Spring	15	3.22	4.44	4.43	5.70	31	2.96	4.26	4.36	6.82
	Summer	18	2.45	3.39	3.44	4.48	14	2.48	4.01	3.86	5.04
	Autumn	17	3.11	3.90	3.92	4.90	14	2.85	4.46	4.41	6.12
	Winter	14	3.54	4.55	4.74	6.08	17	3.60	5.58	5.75	10.4
Spavinaw Creek near Sycamore, Okla. (07191220)	All Seasons	34	2.80	4.50	4.59	7.35	68	3.03	4.75	4.84	9.36
	Spring	12	3.41	4.60	4.67	5.80	29	3.15	4.40	4.64	7.10
	Summer	9	2.80	3.92	3.76	4.40	12	3.03	4.15	4.21	5.48
	Autumn	4	4.21	4.40	4.40	4.60	10	3.58	4.58	4.52	5.50
	Winter	9	4.60	5.36	5.41	7.35	17	3.20	5.70	5.81	9.36
Spavinaw Creek near Colcord, Okla. (071912213)	All Seasons	66	2.20	3.66	3.70	5.84	86	2.08	4.06	4.33	9.62
	Spring	15	2.68	4.10	4.05	5.01	34	2.30	4.00	4.20	6.29
	Summer	19	2.20	3.02	3.12	4.37	16	2.08	3.66	3.83	8.11
	Autumn	18	2.82	3.19	3.49	4.50	18	2.70	3.80	3.94	5.29
	Winter	14	3.21	4.20	4.40	5.84	18	3.80	5.03	5.41	9.62
Beaty Creek near Jay, Okla. (07191222)	All Seasons	53	.67	1.84	2.07	4.10	93	1.13	2.93	3.02	7.27
	Spring	11	1.04	3.00	2.64	4.10	36	1.16	2.97	3.08	7.27
	Summer	13	.89	1.85	1.94	2.80	20	1.70	2.52	2.58	5.12
	Autumn	17	.67	1.16	1.58	3.40	17	1.13	2.83	2.59	4.24
	Winter	12	1.18	2.03	2.40	4.07	20	2.50	3.68	3.70	5.00

runoff samples than in base-flow samples collected only during the winter season from the Cherokee City station. Nitrogen concentrations were significantly greater in runoff samples than in base-flow samples collected during the summer and winter seasons from the Colcord station. No significant difference in nitrogen concentrations was detected between base-flow and runoff samples collected during the spring season from any station.

Nitrogen concentrations in base-flow samples often were significantly greater ($p \leq 0.05$) in samples collected during winter and spring than during summer or autumn seasons. An exception was observed for the Beaty Creek station in which the Kruskal-Wallis test indicated that concentrations in winter base-flow samples were similar to other seasons (fig. 6). Possible explanations for greater nitrogen concentrations in base-flow samples collected during spring and winter than in other seasons may be caused by (1) a lesser uptake of nitrate or ammonium from terrestrial vegetation resulting in increased leaching of nitrate from groundwater, (2) lack of growth of aquatic vegetation that allows nitrogen to build up in the stream during these seasons compared to summer and autumn months, or (3) an increase in fertilizer applications in late winter or early spring, which contributes to greater ammonium and nitrate concentrations in groundwater.

Nitrogen concentrations were significantly greater ($p \leq 0.05$) in runoff samples collected during winter than all other

Table 7.   Summary statistics of total phosphorus concentrations in base-flow and runoff water samples collected at water-quality stations in the Eucha-Spavinaw Basin, Arkansas and Oklahoma, 2002–09.

[Obs, number of observations; mg/L, milligram per liter; P, phosphorus]

Station name (number)	Time period	Base-flow concentrations					Runoff concentrations				
		Obs	Mini-mum	Median	Mean	Maxi-mum	Obs	Mini-mum	Median	Mean	Maxi-mum
				(mg/L as P)					(mg/L as P)		
Spavinaw Creek near Maysville, Ark. (07191160)	All Seasons	63	0.02	0.03	0.03	0.12	70	0.02	0.05	0.17	1.2
	Spring	13	.02	.03	.03	.04	29	.03	.05	.17	.94
	Summer	18	.02	.03	.03	.07	13	.02	.04	.13	.92
	Autumn	16	.02	.03	.03	.06	14	.02	.05	.15	.90
	Winter	16	.02	.02	.03	.12	14	.02	.05	.21	1.2
Spavinaw Creek near Cherokee City, Ark. (07191179)	All Seasons	62	.06	.14	.15	.32	74	.03	.14	.23	1.6
	Spring	15	.06	.11	.13	.23	30	.03	.15	.23	1.6
	Summer	18	.08	.15	.15	.23	15	.03	.14	.21	1.3
	Autumn	15	.07	.16	.18	.32	13	.09	.12	.21	1.1
	Winter	14	.07	.13	.15	.30	16	.07	.13	.24	1.2
Spavinaw Creek near Sycamore, Okla. (07191220)	All Seasons	34	.02	.10	.11	.18	66	.07	.13	.21	1.2
	Spring	11	.08	.11	.11	.15	29	.07	.14	.22	.98
	Summer	10	.08	.11	.11	.15	11	.08	.11	.18	.98
	Autumn	4	.08	.08	.09	.12	10	.08	.12	.14	.24
	Winter	9	.02	.09	.10	.18	16	.07	.11	.24	1.2
Spavinaw Creek near Colcord, Okla. (071912213)	All Seasons	63	.04	.08	.09	.26	85	.06	.12	.24	1.6
	Spring	15	.04	.08	.09	.13	33	.06	.13	.26	1.6
	Summer	19	.06	.08	.09	.15	17	.07	.10	.23	1.5
	Autumn	15	.07	.08	.08	.11	18	.07	.12	.18	.83
	Winter	14	.07	.08	.10	.26	17	.06	.11	.25	1.1
Beaty Creek near Jay, Okla. (07191222)	All Seasons	52	.02	.04	.05	.10	92	.02	.07	.18	1.1
	Spring	10	.03	.04	.04	.07	36	.02	.09	.19	1.1
	Summer	15	.03	.05	.05	.09	20	.04	.07	.13	.89
	Autumn	15	.03	.05	.05	.07	17	.03	.10	.26	1.0
	Winter	12	.02	.04	.04	.10	19	.03	.08	.15	.58

seasons at all four stations tested (fig. 6). Possible explanations for greater nitrogen concentrations in runoff samples collected during winter than in other seasons may be a greater amount of organic nitrogen or ammonium available for runoff in leaf-litter during the previous season or less dilution of nitrate from groundwater because low flow generally is reduced during winter months compared to other seasons (fig. 3). Investigation into the variability or loading of various forms of total nitrogen was beyond the scope of this report but would help in evaluation of possible causes for temporal and flow-related variability of nitrogen concentrations.

Nitrogen concentrations in base-flow samples significantly increased ($p \leq 0.05$) downstream from the Maysville station to the Sycamore station (fig. 5). Nitrogen concentrations in base-flow samples collected from Spavinaw Creek significantly decreased ($p \leq 0.05$) in a downstream direction from the Sycamore station to the Colcord station (fig. 5). Nitrogen concentrations in base-flow samples from stations in the Eucha-Spavinaw Basin generally increased with increasing streamflow (fig. 8). Nitrate can be more prone to leach into groundwater from soils and subsoils than phosphorus (Cooke and Williams, 1970). As base flow increased by addition

Table 8.   Mann-Whitney rank-sum test results comparing base-flow total nitrogen or total phosphorus concentrations to runoff total nitrogen or total phosphorus concentrations from water samples collected at water-quality stations in the Eucha-Spavinaw Basin, 2002–09.

[z-score, normal test statistic with correction for ties; *p*-value, probability value; values in bold indicate statistically significant differences between groups of data at 95-percent confidence level (probability value less than or equal to 0.05); <, less than]

Station name (number)	Time period	Nitrogen		Phosphorus	
		z-score	*p*-value	z-score	*p*-value
Spavinaw Creek near Maysville, Ark. (07191160)	All Seasons	**-4.473**	**<0.0001**	**-6.287**	**<0.0001**
	Spring	.0867	.9309	**-4.233**	**<.0001**
	Summer	**-2.943**	**.0032**	**-2.565**	**.0103**
	Autumn	**-3.391**	**.0007**	**-2.644**	**.0082**
	Winter	**-3.223**	**.0013**	**-2.623**	**.0087**
Spavinaw Creek near Cherokee City, Ark. (07191179)	All Seasons	**-2.284**	**.0224**	-.3256	.7447
	Spring	.6327	.5269	-1.313	.1892
	Summer	-1.862	.0626	.9767	.3287
	Autumn	-1.747	.0806	.2536	.7998
	Winter	**-2.164**	**.0304**	.0208	.9834
Spavinaw Creek near Sycamore, Okla. (07191220)	All Seasons	-.6177	.5368	**-2.58**	**.0099**
	Spring	.5015	.616	**-2.016**	**.0438**
	Summer	NA[1]	NA[1]	.3174	.7509
	Autumn	NA[1]	NA[1]	NA[1]	NA[1]
	Winter	NA[1]	NA[1]	NA[1]	NA[1]
Spavinaw Creek near Colcord, Okla. (071912213)	All Seasons	**-3.047**	**.0023**	**-5.141**	**<.0001**
	Spring	.0326	.974	**-2.904**	**.0037**
	Summer	**-2.054**	**.04**	**-2.219**	**.0265**
	Autumn	-1.788	.0738	**-2.515**	**.0119**
	Winter	**-2.185**	**.0289**	-1.707	.0878
Beaty Creek near Jay, Okla. (07191222)	All Seasons	**-5.031**	**<.0001**	**-6.165**	**<.0001**
	Spring	-.8421	.3997	**-2.73**	**.0063**
	Summer	**-2.415**	**.0157**	**-2.785**	**.0054**
	Autumn	**-3.083**	**.002**	**-3.458**	**.0005**
	Winter	**-2.843**	**.0045**	**-3.469**	**.0005**

[1] The Mann-Whitney rank-sum test was not performed because there were less than 10 base-flow samples available for this season.

of groundwater, additional nitrate in the groundwater may increase the concentration of nitrogen in the stream. Spavinaw Creek received substantial nitrogen concentrations from the Decatur wastewater-treatment plant, but Beaty Creek did not. This difference may be a cause of lesser nitrogen concentrations in base-flow samples collected from the Beaty Creek station compared to the Spavinaw Creek stations (fig. 5).

Nitrogen concentrations in runoff samples collected from Spavinaw Creek were significantly greater for the Sycamore station compared to the upstream Maysville station but significantly decreased from the Sycamore station to the downstream Colcord station (fig. 5). Nitrogen concentrations in runoff samples collected from the Beaty Creek station were significantly less than at all other stations (fig. 5). Nitrogen concentrations in runoff samples collected from all stations generally increased with increasing streamflow (fig. 8). The larger concentrations of nitrogen during runoff likely indicate addition of nitrogen from nonpoint sources.

Phosphorus

Phosphorus concentrations were significantly different ($p \leq 0.05$) between runoff samples and base-flow samples for most stations for the entire period or for individual seasons or both (table 8). Boxplots indicate that nitrogen concentrations were greater in runoff samples than in base-flow samples (figs. 5 and 7) where concentrations were significantly different as a result of the Mann-Whitney test (table 8). However, no significant difference in phosphorus concentrations were detected between base-flow and runoff samples collected from the Cherokee City station during the entire period or during any season (table 8). Phosphorus concentrations also were not significantly different between base-flow and runoff samples collected from the Sycamore station during the summer season and collected from the Colcord station during the winter season (table 8). Phosphorus concentrations were significantly different between base-flow and runoff samples collected from the Maysville station and the Beaty Creek station for all seasons.

Phosphorus concentrations in base-flow samples were generally not significantly different ($p \leq 0.05$) between seasons (fig. 7). An exception was observed for the Maysville station in which the multistage Kruskal-Wallis test indicated that phosphorus concentrations in samples collected during summer and autumn were significantly greater than concentrations in samples collected during spring and winter as indicated in figure 7. Possible explanations for greater phosphorus concentrations in base-flow samples collected from the Maysville station during summer and autumn than during other seasons may be caused by an increased concentration in dissolved phosphorus related to variability in seasonal agricultural activities, nutrient cycling from more frequent and abundant algal blooms in the spring and summer, or increased mobility of inorganic phosphates as a product of soil decomposition that can increase with warmer temperatures. Differences in phosphorus concentrations from samples among seasons may not be observed for other Spavinaw Creek stations because those stations, unlike the Maysville station, are downstream from the Decatur wastewater-treatment plant. The plant is a source of dissolved phosphorus to Spavinaw Creek (Haggard and others, 2001) and may not be subject to substantial seasonal variability in waste discharge. Phosphorus concentrations in runoff samples were not significantly different among seasons for any station (fig. 7). Investigation into the variability or loading of dissolved (inorganic phosphates and total dissolved phosphorus) and sediment-sorbed phosphorus was beyond the scope of this report but would help in evaluation of possible causes for temporal variability of total phosphorus concentrations.

Phosphorus concentrations in base-flow samples collected from Spavinaw Creek significantly increased ($p \leq 0.05$) from the Maysville station to the Cherokee City station perhaps because of discharges from the Decatur wastewater-treatment plant between the two stations (fig. 5). Phosphorus concentrations in base-flow samples collected from Spavinaw Creek significantly decreased ($p \leq 0.05$) from the Cherokee City station to the Colcord station (fig. 7). In Spavinaw Creek, phosphorus concentrations in base-flow samples collected from the Maysville station, Sycamore station, and Colcord station generally did not change with increasing streamflow; whereas, phosphorus concentrations in base-flow samples for the Cherokee City station generally decreased with increasing streamflow (fig. 9). Localized increases in phosphorus

concentrations near point-sources have been reported for other point-source affected streams in the region (Haggard, 2000; Haggard and others, 2001; Tortorelli and Pickup, 2006). As base flow increased by addition of groundwater, dilution likely reduced the concentration of dissolved phosphorus from the Decatur wastewater-treatment plant upstream from the Cherokee City station. Phosphorus concentrations were lesser in base-flow and runoff samples collected from the Beaty Creek station than from the Spavinaw Creek stations downstream from the Maysville station (fig. 5). This difference may be caused by the wastewater discharge that affects Spavinaw Creek.

Phosphorus concentrations in runoff samples were not significantly different among the three downstream stations on Spavinaw Creek but were significantly different between the Maysville station and the Beaty Creek station (fig. 5). Phosphorus concentrations in runoff samples collected from all stations generally increased with increasing streamflow (fig. 9). Larger concentrations of phosphorus present in streams during runoff than during base flow are likely caused by the addition of phosphorus from nonpoint sources, resuspension of phosphorus from the streambed sediment, and streambank erosion. Wagner and Woodruff (1997) and Storm and others (2001) attribute most of the phosphorus transported in the basin to nonpoint sources during runoff.

Estimated Mean Annual Loads

Estimated mean annual nitrogen and phosphorus loads are discussed in this section. Total annual loads are divided into base-flow and runoff components as presented in tables 9–10 and figures 10–11.

Nitrogen

Estimated mean annual nitrogen total loads (the sum of base flow and runoff loads) were substantially greater at Spavinaw Creek stations than at the Beaty Creek station (about two to four times), primarily because of greater streamflow and possibly because of greater nitrogen concentrations in samples collected at the Spavinaw Creek stations (tables 2 and 9, fig. 8). Annual total loads increased in Spavinaw Creek in a downstream direction from the Maysville station to the Colcord station with the annual total load at the Colcord station about twice that of the Maysville station (table 9).

Mean annual base-flow loads at the Spavinaw Creek stations were about five to nine times greater than base-flow loads at the Beaty Creek station (table 9). Annual nitrogen base-flow loads increased in Spavinaw Creek in a downstream direction from the Maysville station to the Colcord station with the annual base-flow load at the Colcord station almost twice that of the Maysville station (table 9).

Estimated mean annual nitrogen runoff loads in the basin increased with increasing drainage area and with increasing streamflow (tables 2 and 9). The runoff component of the

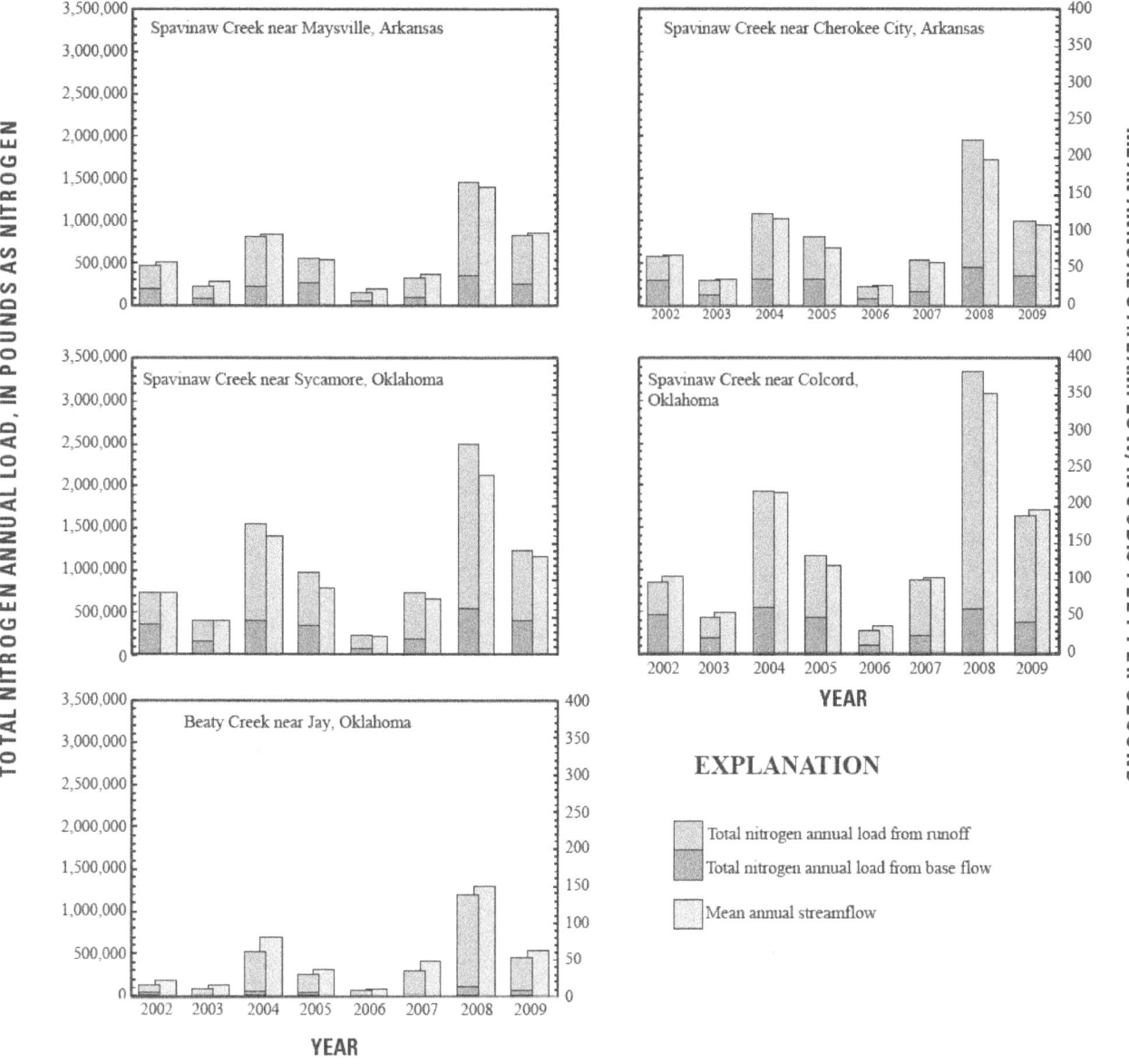

Figure 10. Total nitrogen annual total load, separated by annual load from base flow and annual load from runoff, and mean annual streamflow, at water-quality stations in the Eucha-Spavinaw Basin, Arkansas and Oklahoma, 2002–09.

mean annual nitrogen load for Beaty Creek was 88 percent (table 9). The range in the runoff component of the mean annual nitrogen load at the Spavinaw Creek stations was 67 to 73 percent and increased with increasing drainage area (tables 2 and 9). Runoff was indicated no more than 34 percent of the time for any station (table 11), but accounted for most of the annual nitrogen total load for every station. The fraction of load delivered during runoff on all stations also exceeded the fraction of total flow that is runoff for every station (table 3).

Annual nitrogen total, base-flow, and runoff loads were the greatest during the calendar year 2008 and lowest during the calendar year 2006 for all stations (fig. 10). Increases and decreases in annual nitrogen load correspond strongly

to increases and decreases in mean annual streamflow (fig. 10). This strong correspondence is likely because of the importance of the streamflow in transport of nitrogen and is expressed by the dominance of streamflow terms in estimating daily mean nitrogen load from the S-LOADEST equations (table 4).

Phosphorus

Estimated mean annual phosphorus total loads were substantially greater in Spavinaw Creek from the Cherokee City station to the Colcord station than at the Beaty Creek station, possibly because of greater streamflow and greater phosphorus

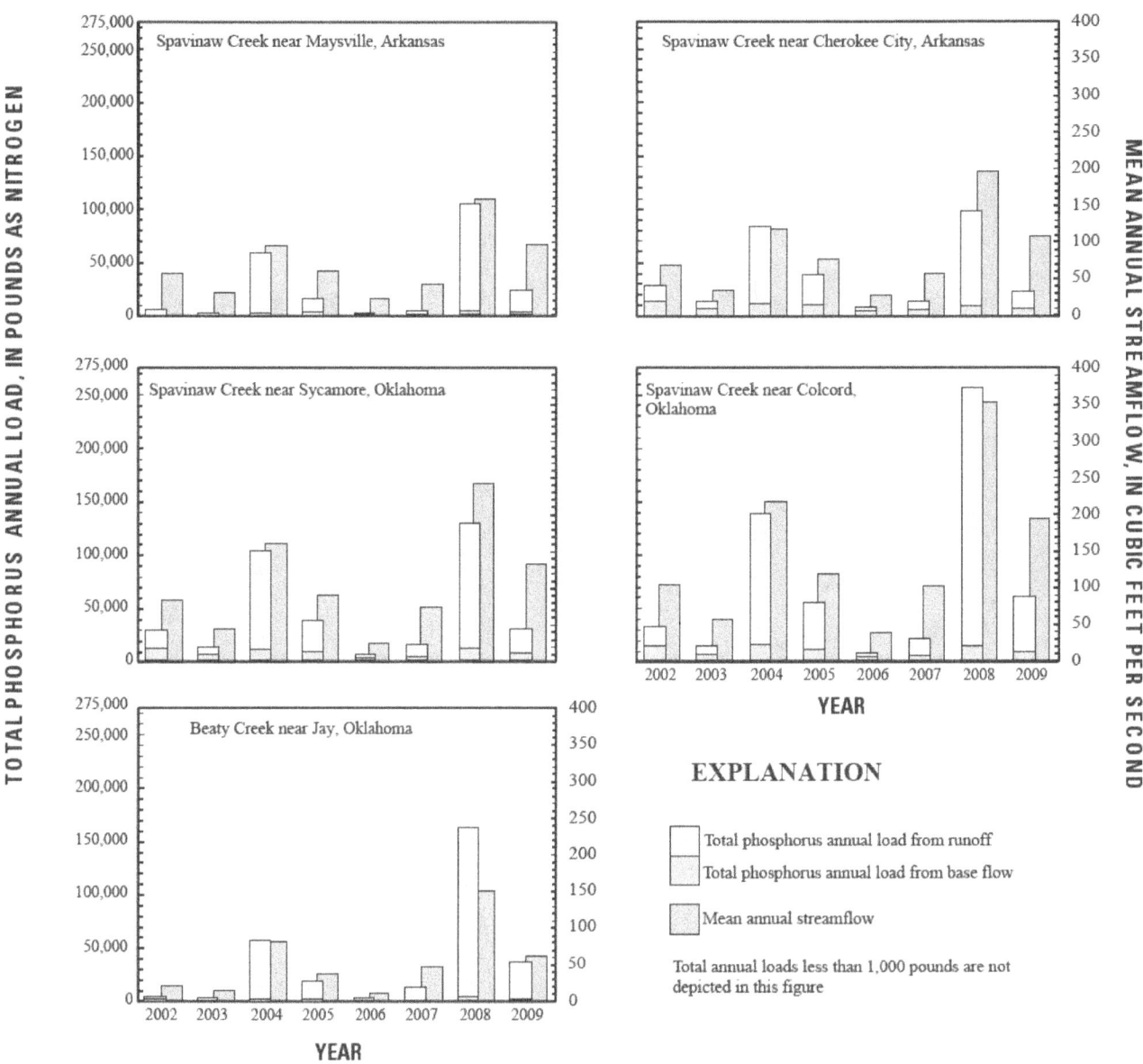

Figure 11. Total phosphorus total annual load, separated by annual load from base flow and annual load from runoff, and mean annual streamflow, at water-quality stations in the Eucha-Spavinaw Basin, Arkansas and Oklahoma, 2002–09.

concentrations at those stations (tables 2, figs. 9 and 10). Mean annual phosphorus total loads were greater at the Beaty Creek station than at the Maysville station on Spavinaw Creek (table 10) even though annual mean streamflow was greater at the Maysville station (table 2). This observation indicated that the difference was likely because of greater phosphorus concentrations at the Beaty Creek station than the Maysville station (fig. 5). Mean annual phosphorus total loads increased in a downstream direction in Spavinaw Creek (table 10) from the Maysville station to the Colcord station; the annual total load at the Colcord station was about three times that of Maysville station (table 10).

Estimated mean annual phosphorus base-flow loads were substantially less in Beaty Creek than in Spavinaw Creek

(table 10). Mean annual phosphorus base-flow loads at the Spavinaw Creek stations were about two to nine times greater than base-flow loads at the Beaty Creek station. Mean annual phosphorus base-flow loads increased substantially in Spavinaw Creek from the Maysville station to the Cherokee City station. This increase was observed perhaps because of inflows from discharges from the Decatur wastewater-treatment plant; the mean annual base-flow load at the Cherokee City station was about four times that of Maysville station (table 10). The mean annual base-flow loads at the three downstream stations on Spavinaw Creek from the Cherokee City station to the Colcord station were similar (table 10).

Estimated mean annual phosphorus runoff loads in the basin increased with increasing drainage area in Spavinaw

Table 9. Estimated mean annual total nitrogen loads and yields by using regression methods from concentrations in water-quality samples collected at water-quality stations in the Eucha-Spavinaw Basin, Arkansas and Oklahoma, for the period 2002–09.

[mi^2, square mile; lb/yr, pound per year; $lb/yr/mi^2$, pound per year per square mile; SEP, standard error of prediction; N, nitrogen; Differences between total load and the sum of the base-flow load plus runoff loads are because of rounding.]

| Station name (number) | Drainage area (mi^2) | Estimated mean annual | | | | | | Load delivered during runoff (percent) |
		Total load[1] (+/- SEP[2]) (lb/yr as N)	Total yield ($lb/yr/mi^2$ as N)	Base-flow load[3] (lb/yr as N)	Base-flow yield ($lb/yr/mi^2$ as N)	Runoff load[4] (lb/yr as N)	Runoff yield ($lb/yr/mi^2$ as N)	
Spavinaw Creek near Maysville, Ark. (07191160)	88.2	604,800 (16,400)	6,850	197,000	2,230	407,800	4,620	67
Spavinaw Creek near Cherokee City, Ark. (07191179)	104	804,000 (15,600)	7,730	260,000	2,500	543,900	5,230	68
Spavinaw Creek near Sycamore, Okla. (07191220)	133	1,041,000 (19,000)	7,830	301,600	2,270	739,200	5,560	71
Spavinaw Creek near Colcord, Okla. (071912213)	163	1,316,000 (27,600)	8,070	360,900	2,210	955,300	5,860	73
Beaty Creek near Jay, Okla. (07191222)	59.2	364,800 (17,900)	6,160	42,100	710	322,700	5,450	88

[1] The mean of annual total load (base flow and runoff) for the study period.

[2] Calculated by S-LOADEST and are statistics of all data.

[3] Means of the base-flow loads are calculated from base-flow days data only.

[4] Means of the runoff loads are calculated from runoff days data only.

Creek (tables 2 and 10). The range in the runoff component of the mean annual phosphorus total load for the Spavinaw Creek stations was 79 to 93 percent (table 10). The mean annual phosphorus load contributed by runoff at the three downstream Spavinaw Creek stations generally increased from the Cherokee City station to the Colcord station (table 10). The runoff component of the mean annual phosphorus total load for Beaty Creek was 98 percent (table 10). Most of the phosphorus loads for Beaty Creek are delivered during runoff, and the mean annual runoff load for Beaty Creek was larger than either of the runoff loads of the two upper Spavinaw Creek stations (table 10). Runoff was indicated no more than 34 percent of the time for any station (table 11), but accounted for most of the annual phosphorus total load for every station (table 10). The phosphorus load delivered during runoff for all stations also substantially exceeded the fraction of total flow that is runoff for every station (table 3). The percentage of the estimated mean annual phosphorus load delivered during

runoff at each station ranged from 9 to 25 percent higher than the percentage of the estimated mean annual nitrogen load delivered during runoff for the same station (tables 9 and 10), that indicates that phosphorus delivery is likely more runoff-driven than nitrogen delivery in the Eucha-Spavinaw Basin. Greater phosphorus delivery and loading during runoff may be because the main source of phosphorus loading was likely from phosphorus-sorption to sediment, which was delivered to the stream during runoff by overland erosion, resuspension of phosphorus from the streambed, or streambank erosion. However, a substantial source of nitrogen loading may be from nitrate delivered to the stream primarily from groundwater.

Similar to annual nitrogen loads, estimated annual phosphorus total, base-flow and runoff loads were the greatest during the calendar year 2008 and least during the calendar year 2006 for all stations (fig. 11). Increases and decreases in annual phosphorus loads generally correspond strongly to increases and decreases in annual mean streamflow (fig. 11).

Table 10. Estimated mean annual total phosphorus loads and yields by using regression methods from concentrations in water-quality samples collected at water-quality stations in the Eucha-Spavinaw Basin, Arkansas and Oklahoma, 2002–09.

[mi², square mile; lb/yr, pound per year; lb/yr/mi², pound per year per square mile; SEP, standard error of prediction; P, phosphorus; Differences between total load and the sum of the base-flow load plus runoff loads are because of rounding.]

Station name (number)	Drainage area (mi²)	Estimated mean annual					Runoff yield (lb/yr/mi² as P)	Load delivered during runoff (percent)
		Total load[1] (+/- SEP[2]) (lb/yr as P)	Total yield (lb/yr/mi² as P)	Base-flow load[3] (lb/yr as P)	Base-flow yield (lb/yr/mi² as P)	Runoff load[4] (lb/yr as P)		
Spavinaw Creek near Maysville, Ark. (07191160)	88.2	26,700 (**3,110**)	300	1,990	20	24,700	280	93
Spavinaw Creek near Chero-kee City, Ark. (07191179)	104	38,000 (**3,530**)	370	8,130	80	29,800	290	79
Spavinaw Creek near Syca-more, Okla. (07191220)	133	44,900 (**3,960**)	330	7,300	50	37,600	280	84
Spavinaw Creek near Col-cord, Okla. (071912213)	163	72,000 (**8,390**)	450	8,990	60	63,000	390	88
Beaty Creek near Jay, Okla. (07191222)	59.2	36,400 (**5,570**)	620	900	20	35,500	600	98

[1] The mean of annual total load (base flow and runoff) for the study period.

[2] Calculated by S-LOADEST and are statistics of all data.

[3] Means of the base-flow loads are calculated from base-flow days data only.

[4] Means of the runoff loads are calculated from runoff days data only.

Like nitrogen loads, this strong correspondence was likely because of the importance of the streamflow in transport of phosphorus and is expressed by the dominance of stream-flow terms in estimating daily mean nitrogen load from the S-LOADEST equations (table 5).

Estimated Mean Seasonal Loads

Estimated mean seasonal nitrogen and phosphorus loads are discussed in this section. Estimated mean seasonal loads are subdivided into base-flow and runoff components (tables 12 and 13).

Nitrogen

Estimated mean seasonal nitrogen base-flow loads generally were least in summer or autumn and greatest in spring at all stations in the Eucha-Spavinaw Basin. Seasonal base-flow loads generally corresponded with mean seasonal streamflow, whereby, mean streamflow also was least in autumn and greatest in spring at all stations (fig. 4). The mean seasonal base-flow loads indicated the same pattern as the annual base-flow loads (tables 9 and 12) in terms of variability among stations. Mean seasonal base-flow loads for the Spavinaw Creek stations were about 4 to 11 times greater than seasonal base-flow loads at the Beaty Creek station (table 12). Mean seasonal nitrogen base-flow loads increased in a downstream direction in Spavinaw Creek from the Maysville station to the Colcord station; the seasonal base-flow load at the Colcord station was about twice that at the Maysville station for any given season (table 12).

Estimated mean seasonal nitrogen runoff loads were least in summer and greatest in spring at all stations for the study period (table 12). In general, seasonal runoff loads corresponded to seasonal streamflow for spring and winter but

Table 11. Number of days of base flow and runoff designated by Base-Flow Index (BFI) program at water-quality stations in the Eucha-Spavinaw Basin, Arkansas and Oklahoma, 2002–09.

[Spring is March through May, Summer is June through August, Autumn is September through November, and Winter is December through February]

Station name (number)	Seasons								Total for all seasons during 2002–09		Percent of runoff days for 2002–09
	Spring		Summer		Autumn		Winter				
	Base flow	Runoff	Base flow	Runoff	Base flow	Runoff	Base flow	Runoff	Base flow	Runoff	
Spavinaw Creek near Maysville, Ark. (07191160)	440	296	585	151	597	131	515	207	2,137	785	27
Spavinaw Creek near Cherokee City, Ark. (07191179)	437	299	575	161	575	153	499	223	2,086	836	29
Spavinaw Creek near Sycamore, Okla. (07191220)	425	311	574	162	568	160	472	250	2,039	883	30
Spavinaw Creek near Colcord, Okla. (071912213)	439	297	559	177	540	188	472	250	2,010	912	31
Beaty Creek near Jay, Okla. (07191222)	395	341	528	208	585	143	433	289	1,941	981	34

Table 12. Estimated mean seasonal total nitrogen base-flow and runoff loads estimated by using regression methods from concentrations in water-quality samples collected at water-quality stations in the Eucha-Spavinaw Basin, Arkansas and Oklahoma, 2002–09.

[Values are loads in pound per season as nitrogen; Spring is March through May, Summer is June through August, Autumn is September through November, and Winter is December through February]

Flow type	Station name (number)	Estimated mean seasonal total nitrogen load			
		Spring	Summer	Autumn	Winter
Base flow	Spavinaw Creek near Maysville, Ark. (07191160)	63,100	41,100	39,640	53,100
	Spavinaw Creek near Cherokee City, Ark. (07191179)	85,800	52,700	53,300	68,400
	Spavinaw Creek near Sycamore, Okla. (07191220)	102,300	65,900	58,600	74,800
	Spavinaw Creek near Colcord, Okla. (071912213)	125,000	69,000	68,600	98,100
	Beaty Creek near Jay, Okla. (07191222)	17,600	6,550	7,310	10,600
Runoff	Spavinaw Creek near Maysville, Ark. (07191160)	196,000	52,550	64,400	110,500
	Spavinaw Creek near Cherokee City, Ark. (07191179)	245,000	68,200	72,000	167,700
	Spavinaw Creek near Sycamore, Okla. (07191220)	322,000	96,500	115,000	234,000
	Spavinaw Creek near Colcord, Okla. (071912213)	422,000	125,000	141,000	284,000
	Beaty Creek near Jay, Okla. (07191222)	132,000	48,200	60,600	96,800

not summer and autumn. Summer runoff loads were slightly less than autumn runoff loads even though mean summer streamflow was slightly greater than mean autumn stream-flow (fig. 4), indicating that differences in the loads between these seasons may be caused by differences in concentration rather than streamflow. Summer and autumn concentrations in runoff samples were similar at Spavinaw Creek stations (although autumn concentrations were greater than summer concentrations at the Beaty Creek station, fig. 6). Even though mean nitrogen concentrations in runoff samples were not significantly different ($p \leq 0.05$) between summer and autumn seasons for stations on Spavinaw Creek, the upper end of the distribution in nitrogen concentrations in runoff samples was

greater in autumn than in summer at Spavinaw Creek stations (fig. 6). These slight differences in seasonal concentrations may be the reason for the lesser summer loads compared to autumn loads.

Estimated mean seasonal nitrogen runoff loads increased with increasing drainage area (tables 2 and 12) and with increasing streamflow (fig. 4) indicating the same pattern as annual runoff loads (table 9).

Phosphorus

Estimated mean seasonal phosphorus base-flow loads were greatest in spring for all stations, but minimum seasonal

Table 13.   Estimated mean seasonal total phosphorus base-flow and runoff loads estimated by using regression methods from concentrations in water-quality samples collected at water-quality stations in the Eucha-Spavinaw basin, Arkansas and Oklahoma, 2002–09.

[Values are loads in pound per season as phosphorus; Spring is March through May, Summer is June through August, Autumn is September through November, and Winter is December through February]

Flow type	Station name (number)	Estimated mean seasonal total phosphorus load			
		Spring	Summer	Autumn	Winter
Base flow	Spavinaw Creek near Maysville, Ark. (07191160)	660	519	408	403
	Spavinaw Creek near Cherokee City, Ark. (07191179)	2,300	2,120	1,830	1,880
	Spavinaw Creek near Sycamore, Okla. (07191220)	2,520	1,950	1,290	1,540
	Spavinaw Creek near Colcord, Okla. (071912213)	3,200	2,220	1,600	1,960
	Beaty Creek near Jay, Okla. (07191222)	368	170	180	180
Runoff	Spavinaw Creek near Maysville, Ark. (07191160)	12,800	6,250	2,800	3,550
	Spavinaw Creek near Cherokee City, Ark. (07191179)	13,500	7,200	2,400	6,990
	Spavinaw Creek near Sycamore, Okla. (07191220)	18,000	8,780	3,520	8,110
	Spavinaw Creek near Colcord, Okla. (071912213)	32,000	12,500	6,900	12,500
	Beaty Creek near Jay, Okla. (07191222)	10,700	6,890	7,540	12,200

base-flow loads varied among stations. Mean seasonal phosphorus base-flow loads were least in autumn at the Cherokee City, Sycamore, and Colcord stations on Spavinaw Creek, least in winter at Spavinaw Creek near Maysville, and least in summer at the Beaty Creek station (table 13). The variability of mean seasonal base-flow loads among stations had a similar pattern to the annual base-flow loads (tables 10 and 13). Mean seasonal phosphorus base-flow loads were substantially less in Beaty Creek than in the Spavinaw Creek stations (table 13). Mean seasonal base-flow loads at stations on Spavinaw Creek were about 2 to 13 times greater than base-flow loads at the station on Beaty Creek (table 13). Mean seasonal phosphorus base-flow loads in Spavinaw Creek increased substantially from the Maysville station to the Cherokee City station, perhaps because of the inflow of wastewater discharges from the Decatur wastewater-treatment plant; the mean seasonal loads at the Cherokee City station were about three and one-half to five times that at the Maysville station for any given season (table 13). The mean seasonal base-flow loads at the three downstream stations on Spavinaw Creek from Cherokee City to Colcord were similar (table 13). However, mean summer, mean autumn, and mean winter base-flow loads were greater at the Cherokee City station than at the Sycamore station on Spavinaw Creek. As base flow increased by addition of groundwater, dilution may have reduced the load of phosphorus from point sources.

Similar to estimated mean seasonal phosphorus base-flow loads, estimated mean seasonal phosphorus runoff loads generally were least in autumn and greatest in spring at most stations. An exception was observed for the Beaty Creek station where mean runoff phosphorus loads were less in summer than in autumn (table 13). Seasonal phosphorus loads from runoff generally corresponded to seasonal streamflow. However, at Beaty Creek, mean summer streamflow was slightly greater than mean autumn streamflow (fig. 4) even though the mean summer phosphorus runoff load was less during summer than autumn. Even though mean phosphorus concentrations in runoff samples were not significantly different between summer and autumn seasons for the Beaty Creek station, the upper end of the distribution in phosphorus concentrations in runoff samples was greater in autumn than in summer (fig. 7). These slight differences in seasonal concentrations may be the reason for the lesser mean summer load compared to autumn load for the Beaty Creek station.

Estimated mean seasonal phosphorus runoff loads in the basin generally increased with increasing drainage area and with increasing streamflow at the Spavinaw Creek stations (fig. 4 and table 13). Much of the phosphorus loads at the Beaty Creek station were delivered during runoff (table 10), and autumn and winter runoff phosphorus loads at the Beaty Creek station generally were larger than loads at some of the Spavinaw Creek stations (table 13).

Estimated Mean Annual Yields

Estimated mean annual nitrogen and phosphorus yields are discussed in this section. Total annual yields are divided into base-flow and runoff components.

Nitrogen

Estimated mean annual nitrogen total yields generally increased slightly in a downstream direction in Spavinaw Creek (table 9). The estimated mean annual nitrogen total yields in Spavinaw Creek ranged from 6,850 to 8,070 pounds per year per square mile (lbs/yr/mi^2); the greatest yield was reported for the Colcord station, and the least yield was reported for the Maysville station (table 9). An even lesser yield was calculated for the Beaty Creek station (6,160 lbs/yr/mi^2) than for the Maysville station. No substantial point source was contributing nitrogen to Spavinaw Creek at the Maysville station, therefore, a possible explanation for the difference between yields at these stations could be a greater application rate of fertilizer, notably from poultry litter, in the Spavinaw Basin (Storm and others, 2002).

Estimated mean annual nitrogen base-flow yields in Spavinaw Creek were similar between the Maysville, Sycamore, and Colcord stations (ranging from 2,210 to 2,270 lbs/yr/mi^2), and slightly greater at the Cherokee City station (2,500 lbs/yr/mi^2). The mean base-flow yield at the Beaty Creek station (710 lbs/yr/mi^2) was about one-third of the mean base-flow yields of the Spavinaw Creek stations (table 9). Possible explanations for this difference in base-flow yield may be a greater influence of groundwater on streamflow and greater nitrogen base-flow concentrations at Spavinaw Creek (downstream from the Maysville station) than Beaty Creek (tables 3 and 9), and, therefore, a greater percentage of nitrogen load delivered during base flow for Spavinaw Creek compared to Beaty Creek (table 9).

Estimated mean annual nitrogen runoff yields in Spavinaw Creek generally increased from the Maysville to the Colcord station, ranging from 4,620 to 5,860 lbs/yr/mi^2 (table 9). Unlike mean annual base-flow yields, Beaty Creek mean annual runoff yields were similar to runoff yields in Spavinaw Creek (5,450 lbs/yr/mi^2) (table 9).

Phosphorus

Estimated mean annual phosphorus total yields in Spavinaw Creek generally increased in a downstream direction, ranging from 300 to 450 lbs/yr/mi^2; the greatest yield was reported for the Colcord station, and the least yield was reported for the Maysville station (table 10). The mean total phosphorus yield for Beaty Creek (620 lbs/yr/mi^2) was greater than for any Spavinaw Creek station.

Estimated mean annual phosphorus base-flow yield was substantially less in Beaty Creek (20 lbs/yr/mi^2) than in the three downstream Spavinaw Creek stations (50 to 80 lbs/yr/mi^2) but was the same as the Maysville station (table 10). Mean annual phosphorus base-flow yield increased substantially in Spavinaw Creek from the Maysville station to the Cherokee City station (table 10); the mean annual base-flow yield at the Cherokee City station was four times that of the Maysville station (table 10). Mean annual phosphorus base-flow yields decreased slightly from the Cherokee City station

to the Colcord station. This variability of base-flow yield among stations probably happened because of the inflow of wastewater discharges from the Decatur wastewater-treatment plant between the Maysville station and Cherokee City station and yields decreased downstream from the Cherokee City station by addition of groundwater, resulting in dilution of phosphorus from the point source.

Estimated mean annual phosphorus runoff yields in Spavinaw Creek were similar at the Maysville station, the Cherokee City station, and the Sycamore station, ranging from 280 to 290 lbs/yr/mi^2. Estimated mean annual phosphorus runoff yields increased slightly to 390 lbs/yr/mi^2 at the Colcord station. The mean runoff yield for the Beaty Creek station (600 lbs/yr/mi^2) was greater than runoff yields for any Spavinaw Creek station (table 11).

The greater total and runoff phosphorus yield in Beaty Creek compared to Spavinaw Creek may be caused by a greater contribution of nonpoint sources of phosphorus in Beaty Creek, resuspension of phosphorus from the streambed, and streambank erosion. The greater runoff yield in Beaty Creek compared to Spavinaw Creek also may be caused by a lesser amount of groundwater contributions to streamflow and a greater percentage of phosphorus load delivered during runoff for Beaty Creek compared to Spavinaw Creek (table 10).

Although substantial differences in mean annual phosphorus runoff yield were detected between Beaty Creek and Spavinaw Creek, no substantial differences in estimated mean annual nitrogen runoff yield were detected between creeks. Because Beaty Creek is more runoff-driven than Spavinaw Creek, this observation further supports the concept that phosphorus delivery is more runoff-driven than nitrogen delivery in the Eucha-Spavinaw Basin.

Estimated Mean Flow-Weighted Concentrations

Nitrogen

Estimated mean flow-weighted nitrogen concentrations (mean nitrogen load divided by mean streamflow times a conversion factor) for stations in the basin ranged from 3.49 to 4.94 mg/L as nitrogen (table 14, fig. 12). These concentrations were about 13 to 19 times greater than the median flow-weighted concentration (0.26 mg/L) for stations in mostly undeveloped basins of the United States and were about 7 to 10 times greater than the 75th percentile of flow-weighted nitrogen concentrations in undeveloped basins (0.50 mg/L, Clark and others, 2000) (fig. 12, table 14).

Estimated mean flow-weighted nitrogen concentrations for each station in the basin were consistently greater than the median instantaneous nitrogen concentrations in samples collected from each station shown in figure 12. A varied range of total nitrogen concentrations were observed (table 6, appendixes 1–5). Greater nitrogen concentrations in samples

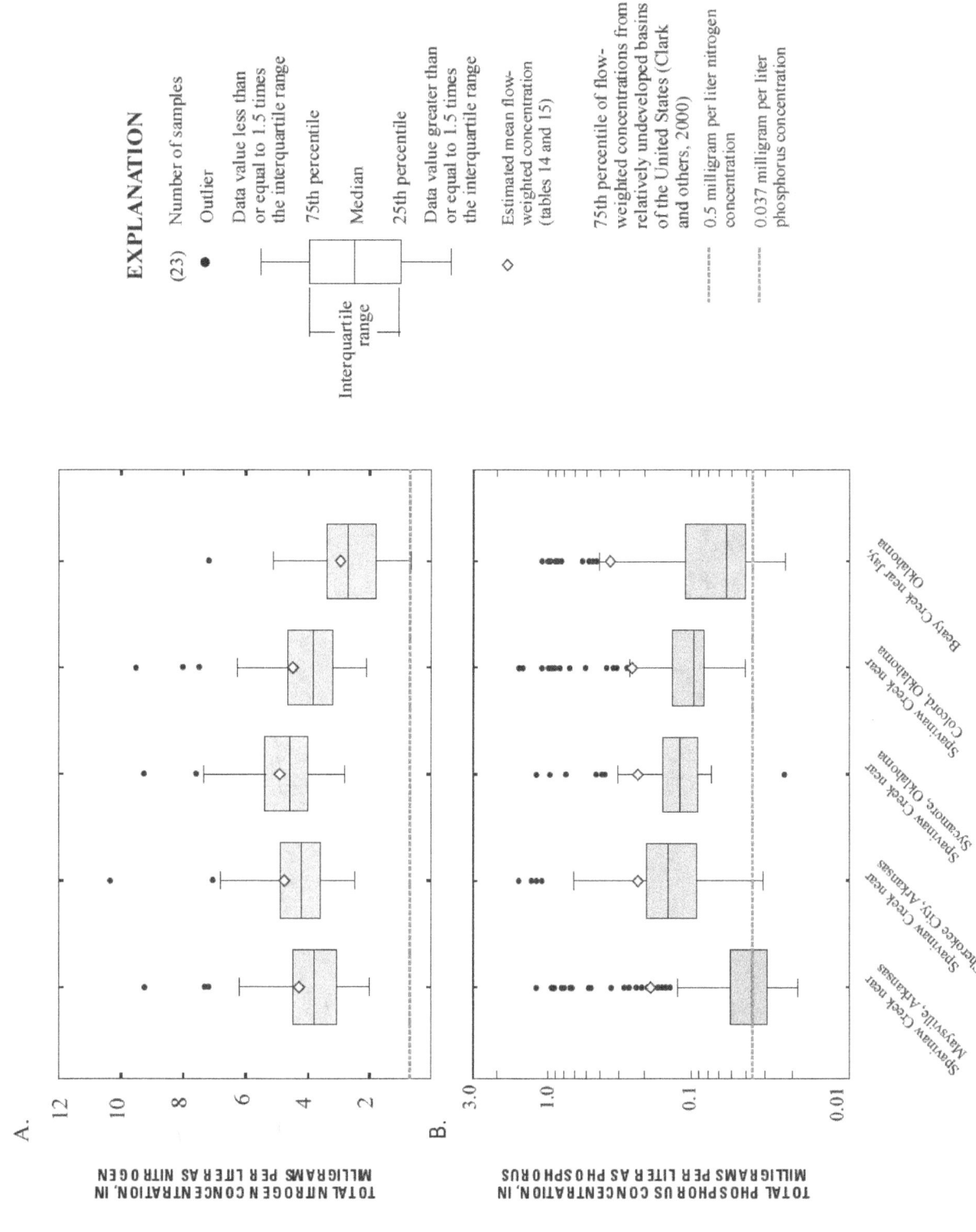

Figure 12. Instantaneous and estimated mean flow-weighted (A) total nitrogen and (B) total phosphorus concentrations in water samples collected at water-quality stations in the Eucha-Spavinaw Basin, Arkansas and Oklahoma, 2002–09.

Table 14. Estimated mean annual total nitrogen loads, mean annual streamflows, and estimated mean flow-weighted total nitrogen concentrations at water-quality stations in the Eucha-Spavinaw Basin, Arkansas and Oklahoma, 2002–09.

[lb/yr, pound per year; ft³/s, cubic foot per second; mg/L, milligram per liter; N, nitrogen.]

Station name (number)	Estimated mean annual total nitrogen load (lb/yr as N)	Mean annual streamflow (ft³/s)	Estimated mean flow-weighted total nitrogen concentration (mg/L as N)
Spavinaw Creek near Maysville, Ark. (07191160)	604,800	71.0	4.33
Spavinaw Creek near Cherokee City, Ark. (07191179)	804,000	86.9	4.70
Spavinaw Creek near Sycamore, Okla. (07191220)	1,041,000	107	4.94
Spavinaw Creek near Colcord, Okla. (071912213)	1,316,000	149	4.49
Beaty Creek near Jay, Okla. (07191222)	364,800	53.1	3.49

collected during runoff can greatly affect the computation of the mean flow-weighted concentrations. For example, the maximum concentration during 2005 at the Colcord station (9.62 mg/L, table 6, appendix 4) was collected during substantial runoff in January 2005 and contributed to a large nitrogen load (appendix 4). Because mean flow-weighted concentration is proportional to load, the result was a large estimated mean flow-weighted nitrogen concentration.

Phosphorus

Estimated mean flow-weighted phosphorus concentrations at stations in the basin ranged from 0.19 to 0.35 mg/L as phosphorus (table 15). These concentrations were 9 to 16 times greater than the median flow-weighted concentration (0.022 mg/L) in mostly undeveloped basins of the United States and were about 5 to 9 times greater than the 75th percentile of flow-weighted phosphorus concentrations

in undeveloped basins (0.037 mg/L, Clark and others, 2000; fig. 12, table 15).

Similar to estimated mean flow-weighted nitrogen concentrations, estimated mean flow-weighted phosphorus concentrations at each station were consistently greater than the median instantaneous phosphorus concentrations shown in figure 12. The phosphorus data have a varied range (table 6, appendixes 1–5). High phosphorus concentrations in samples collected during runoff can greatly affect the computation of the mean flow-weighted concentrations. For example, the maximum concentration during May 2009 at the Beaty Creek station (1.1 mg/L, table 7, appendix 5) was collected during substantial runoff and contributed to a large phosphorus load. However, the greatest daily mean streamflow and load was during a January 2008 event (table 2) with a concentration of 0.58 mg/L (appendix 5) and was responsible for a large proportion of the mean annual load at the Beaty Creek station.

Table 15. Estimated mean annual total phosphorus loads, mean annual streamflows, and estimated mean flow-weighted total phosphorus concentrations at water-quality stations in the Eucha-Spavinaw Basin, Arkansas and Oklahoma, 2002–09.

[lb/yr, pound per year; ft³/s, cubic foot per second; mg/L, milligram per liter; P, phosphorus.]

Station name (number)	Estimated mean annual total phosphorus load (lb/yr as P)	Mean annual streamflow (ft³/s)	Estimated mean flow-weighted total phosphorus concentration (mg/L as P)
Spavinaw Creek near Maysville, Ark. (07191160)	26,700	71.0	0.19
Spavinaw Creek near Cherokee City, Ark. (07191179)	38,000	86.9	.22
Spavinaw Creek near Sycamore, Okla. (07191220)	44,900	107	.21
Spavinaw Creek near Colcord, Okla. (071912213)	72,000	149	.25
Beaty Creek near Jay, Okla. (07191222)	36,400	53.1	.35

A.

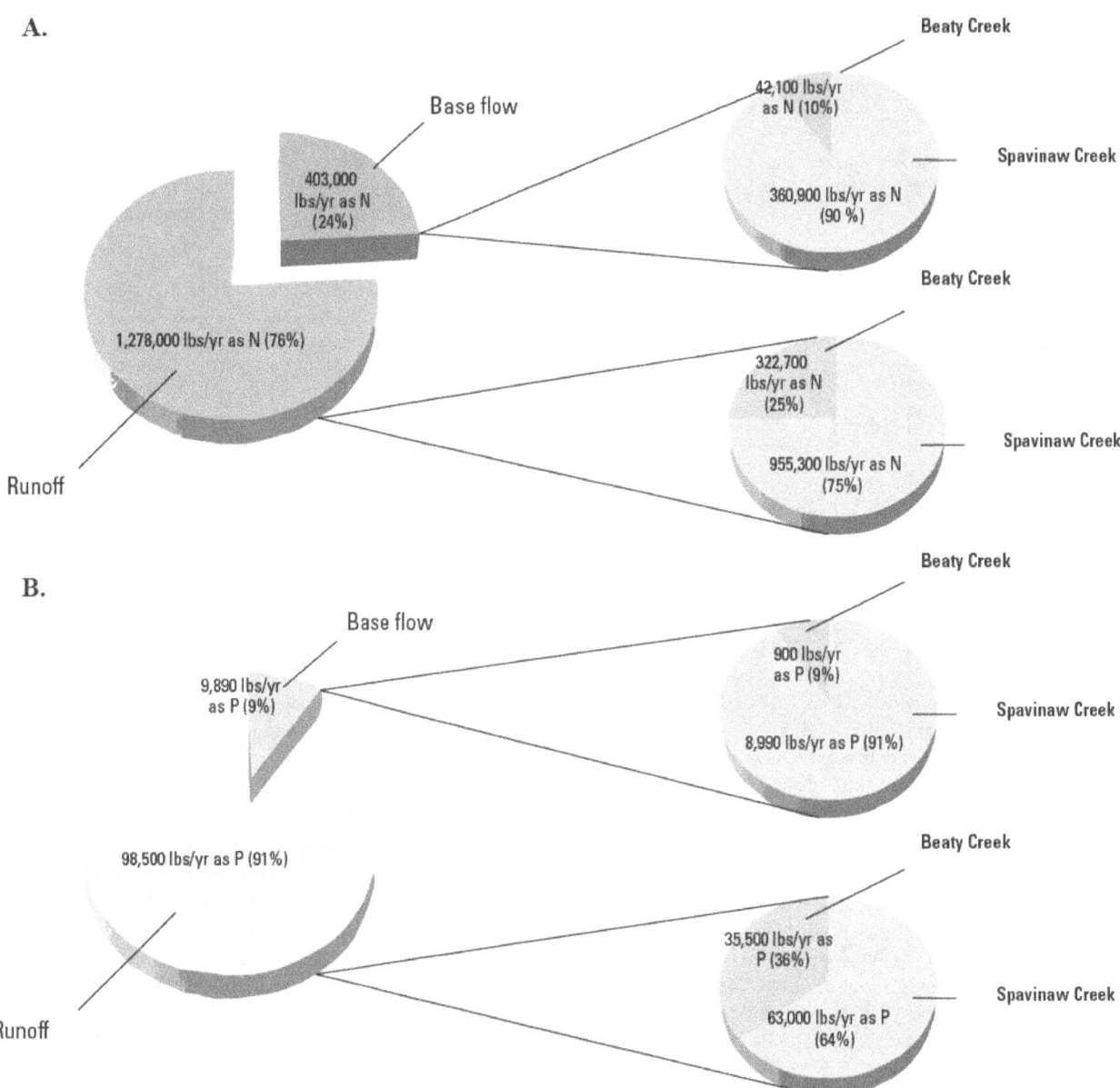

B.

Figure 13.   Graph showing percentage of estimated mean annual (A) total nitrogen and (B) total phosphorus load to Lake Eucha, for the period 2002-09, that is from base flow and from runoff, and the percentage of load contributed from Beaty Creek near Jay, Oklahoma (USGS station identifier 07191222) and Spavinaw Creek near Colcord, Oklahoma (USGS station identifier 071912213).

Estimated Mean Annual Nutrient Loads into Lake Eucha

Much of the mean annual nutrient loads entering Lake Eucha can be estimated by adding the loads for the Beaty Creek station and the Colcord station on Spavinaw Creek. Nutrient loads at these stations do not represent the entire nutrient load into Lake Eucha, but the drainage area upstream from these stations accounts for about 62 percent of the drainage basin upstream from the lake.

Spavinaw Creek and Beaty Creek contributed a mean annual nitrogen total load of 1,681,000 pounds per year

(lbs/yr) (table 16) and 76 percent of the annual nitrogen total load was transported to Lake Eucha by runoff (fig. 13). Spavinaw Creek transported about nine times more nitrogen load during base flow and about three times more nitrogen load during runoff to the lake than did Beaty Creek (table 9).

Spavinaw Creek and Beaty Creek contributed a mean annual phosphorus total load of 108,390 lbs/yr (table 16); 91 percent of the mean annual phosphorus total load was transported to Lake Eucha by runoff (fig. 13). Spavinaw Creek transported about 10 times more phosphorus load during base flow and about 2 times more phosphorus load during runoff to the lake than did Beaty Creek (table 10). The ratio of nitrogen

Table 16. Summary of estimated mean annual total nitrogen and total phosphorus loads to Lake Eucha, Oklahoma, 2002–09.

[lb/yr, pound per year; N, nitrogen; P, phosphorus]

Flow type	Lake Eucha mean annual nitrogen load[1]		Spavinaw Creek near Colcord, Okla. component of mean annual nitrogen load (percent)	Beaty Creek near Jay, Okla. component of mean annual nitrogen load (percent)	Lake Eucha mean annual phosphorus load		Spavinaw Creek near Colcord, Okla. component of mean annual phosphorus load (percent)	Beaty Creek near Jay, Okla. component of mean annual phosphorus load (percent)
	(lb/yr as N)	(percent)			(lb/yr as P)	(percent)		
Base flow[2]	403,000	24	90	10	9,890	9	91	9
Runoff[3]	1,278,000	76	75	25	98,500	91	64	36
Total[4]	1,681,000	100	78	22	108,390	100	66	34

[1] Loads to Lake Eucha are calculated by adding loads from Spavinaw Creek near Colcord, Okla. to loads from Beaty Creek near Jay, Okla. (tables 9 and 10). These two locations account for 62 percent of drainage area that inflows to Lake Eucha.

[2] Means of the base-flow loads are calculated from base-flow day data only by S-LOADEST and are statistics of all data from 2002–09.

[3] Means of the runoff loads are calculated from runoff day data only by S-LOADEST and are statistics of all data from 2002–09.

[4] Differences between total load and the sum of the base-flow load plus runoff loads are because of rounding.

to phosphorus annual loads for the basin was about 15.5:1. The ratio of nitrogen to phosphorus base-flow load for the basin was about 41:1 but was reduced to about 13:1 for runoff load that indicated phosphorus loads were increased relative to nitrogen loads during runoff. The total ratio of the total nitrogen concentration to the total phosphorus concentration in samples collected from Spavinaw and Beaty Creeks generally were greater than 20 for most samples (appendixes 1–5), which may indicate phosphorus is a limiting nutrient for eutrophication in the basin. Because phosphorus was the limiting nutrient in Lake Eucha and Spavinaw Lake, delivery of increased total phosphorus compared to total nitrogen during runoff may increase the risk of algal blooms in the lakes. Total phosphorus likely is less bioavailable than total nitrogen in the basin because a large part of total phosphorus loads are bound to sediment, whereas a major component of total nitrogen are dissolved nitrates, but dissolved nitrogen components were not analyzed. Evaluation of the ratio of nitrogen to phosphorus loads for dissolved or bioavailable components would be a better indicator of eutrophication potential in the lake, but was beyond the scope of this report.

Annual nitrogen and phosphorus loads and the percentage of total load contributed during runoff computed by using data from 2002–09 were greater than the loads reported in Tortorelli (2008) that used data from 2002–06. The mean annual nitrogen total load reported in Tortorelli (2008) ranged from 1,350,000 to 1,490,000 lbs/yr and ranged from 65 to 72 percent of the annual nitrogen total load transported to Lake Eucha during runoff. The mean annual phosphorus total load reported in Tortorelli (2008) ranged from 77,000 to 88,700

lbs/yr and ranged from 86 to 89 percent of the annual phosphorus total load transported to Lake Eucha during runoff. The greater annual total loads computed by using data from 2002–09 could be attributed to substantially greater streamflow in calendar year 2008 than other years. Greater streamflow in 2008 also could have contributed to greater average contribution of runoff to total flow for the period 2002–09 compared to 2002–06.

Summary

The city of Tulsa, Oklahoma, uses Lake Eucha and Spavinaw Lake in the Eucha-Spavinaw Basin in northwestern Arkansas and northeastern Oklahoma for public water supply. The city has spent millions of dollars from 1998–2005 to eliminate taste and odor problems in the drinking water from the Eucha-Spavinaw system, that may be attributable to blue-green algae. Increases in algal biomass in the lakes may be attributable to increases in nutrient concentrations in the lakes and in the waters feeding the lakes.

In July 2001, the U.S. Geological Survey, in cooperation with the City of Tulsa municipal agency, supplemented fixed period, monthly water-quality sampling with six runoff samplings per year for four stations along Spavinaw Creek and one station on Beaty Creek to better determine water quality during a range of streamflows in the basin. Nitrogen and phosphorus concentrations, loads, and yields were determined for the period January 2002 through December 2009 to update a previous report that used data from water-quality samples collected from January 2002 through December 2006.

Nitrogen concentrations were significantly greater ($p \leq 0.05$) in runoff samples than in base-flow samples for the entire period collected from Spavinaw Creek near Maysville and near Cherokee City, Arkansas; Spavinaw Creek near Colcord, Oklahoma, and Beaty Creek near Jay, Oklahoma. Significant differences in nitrogen concentrations in base-flow and runoff samples were variable by season and station. No significant difference in nitrogen concentrations were detected between base-flow and runoff samples collected from any station during the spring season. Nitrogen concentrations in base-flow and runoff samples were most often statistically greater in samples collected during winter and spring than summer or autumn seasons. Nitrogen concentrations in samples collected from all stations generally increased with increasing stream-flow. Greater concentrations of nitrogen in samples collected during runoff than during base flow may indicate addition of nitrogen from nonpoint sources.

Nitrogen concentrations in base-flow and runoff samples collected in Spavinaw Creek significantly increased ($p \leq 0.05$) downstream from the Maysville station to the Sycamore station and then significantly decreased downstream from the Sycamore station to the Colcord station. Nitrogen concentrations in base-flow and runoff samples collected from Beaty Creek were significantly less than in base-flow and runoff samples collected from Spavinaw Creek.

Phosphorus concentrations were significantly greater ($p \leq 0.05$) in runoff samples than in base-flow samples collected from all stations for the entire period except from the Cherokee City station. Significant differences in phosphorus concentrations in base-flow and runoff samples were variable by season and station. Phosphorus concentrations were significantly different between base-flow and runoff samples collected from the Maysville station and the Beaty Creek station for all seasons. The larger concentration of phosphorus in samples collected during runoff likely indicates phosphorus resuspension, stream bank erosion, or addition of phosphorus from nonpoint sources. Phosphorus concentrations in base-flow samples were not significantly different among seasons at most stations. Phosphorus concentrations in runoff samples were not significantly different among seasons for any station.

Phosphorus concentrations in base-flow samples collected from Spavinaw Creek significantly increased ($p \leq 0.05$) from the Maysville station to the Cherokee City station, perhaps because of municipal wastewater discharge between those stations, and then significantly decreased downstream from the Cherokee City station to the Colcord station. Phosphorus concentrations in base-flow samples collected from Beaty Creek were significantly less than phosphorus concentrations in base-flow samples collected from Spavinaw Creek downstream from the Maysville station.

Estimated mean annual nitrogen total and base-flow loads were substantially greater at the Spavinaw Creek stations than at the Beaty Creek station and increased downstream from the Maysville station to the Colcord station on Spavinaw Creek. The runoff component of the annual nitrogen total load for

Beaty Creek was 88 percent; at the Spavinaw Creek stations, the range in the runoff component was 67 to 73 percent. Annual nitrogen total, base-flow, and runoff loads were greatest during the calendar year 2008, and least during the calendar year 2006, the years with the greatest and least mean annual streamflow, respectively.

Estimated mean annual phosphorus total loads were greater at the Spavinaw Creek stations from the Cherokee City station to the Colcord station than at the Beaty Creek station and increased downstream from the Maysville station to the Colcord station in Spavinaw Creek. Estimated mean annual phosphorus base-flow loads at the Spavinaw Creek stations were about two to nine times greater than at the Beaty Creek station. Phosphorus base-flow loads increased downstream by a factor of four from the Maysville station to the Cherokee City station in Spavinaw Creek, perhaps because of the inflow of discharges from the Decatur wastewater-treatment plant. The runoff component of the annual phosphorus total load for Beaty Creek was 98 percent; whereas, at the Spavinaw Creek stations, the range in the runoff component was 79 to 93 percent. Similar to annual nitrogen loads, annual phosphorus total, base-flow, and runoff loads were the greatest during the calendar year 2008 and least during the calendar year 2006.

Estimated mean seasonal nitrogen base-flow loads generally were least in autumn and greatest in spring and estimated mean seasonal nitrogen runoff loads generally were least in summer and greatest in spring. Estimated mean seasonal phosphorus base-flow and runoff loads generally were least in autumn and greatest in spring at all stations with the exception of the Beaty Creek station in which phosphorus base-flow loads were least in summer.

Estimated mean annual nitrogen total yields generally increased in a downstream direction in Spavinaw Creek and ranged from 6,850 to 8,070 pounds per year per square mile. A lesser yield was calculated for the Beaty Creek station (6,160 pounds per year per square mile) than for the Maysville station (6,850 pounds per year per square mile). Estimated mean annual nitrogen base-flow yields ranged from 710 to 2,500 pounds per year per square mile with the least yield at the Beaty Creek station; similar yields among the Maysville station, the Sycamore station, and the Colcord station; and the greatest yield at the Cherokee City station. The nitrogen base-flow yields at all stations on Spavinaw Creek were about three times greater than at the Beaty Creek station. The estimated mean annual nitrogen runoff yields ranged from 4,620 to 5,860 pounds per year per square mile.

Estimated mean annual phosphorus total yields ranged from 300 to 620 pounds per year per square mile. The greatest phosphorus total yield was at the Beaty Creek station, and the least phosphorus total yield was at the Maysville station in Spavinaw Creek. Estimated mean annual phosphorus base-flow yields at the three downstream Spavinaw Creek stations ranged from 50 to 80 pounds per year per square mile. Estimated mean annual phosphorus base-flow yields were the same at the Maysville station in Spavinaw Creek and the Beaty Creek station. Mean annual base-flow yields were greater at the three downstream stations on Spavinaw Creek than at the Beaty Creek station, and were greater at the Cherokee City station than at the Maysville station, probably because of the inflow of discharges from the Decatur wastewater-treatment plant between the stations. Estimated mean annual phosphorus runoff yields ranged from 280 to 390 pounds per year per square mile at stations on Spavinaw Creek, and the mean runoff yield for Beaty Creek was 600 pounds per year per square mile. The greater yield in Beaty Creek than Spavinaw Creek may be caused by a greater contribution of nonpoint sources of phosphorus in Beaty Creek, or greater rates of resuspension of phosphorus from the streambed and greater rates of streambank erosion. The greater runoff yield in Beaty Creek compared to Spavinaw Creek also may be related to a lesser influence of groundwater on streamflow for Beaty Creek compared to Spavinaw Creek.

Estimated mean flow-weighted nitrogen concentrations at all stations in the basin were about 7 to 10 times greater than the 75th percentile of flow-weighted nitrogen concentrations (0.50 milligram per liter) at stations in mostly undeveloped basins of the United States. Estimated mean flow-weighted phosphorus concentrations at all stations in the basin for all three periods were about five to nine times greater than the 75th percentile of flow-weighted phosphorus concentrations (0.037 milligram per liter) at stations in mostly undeveloped basins of the United States.

Spavinaw Creek and Beaty Creek contributed an estimated mean annual nitrogen total load of 1,681,000 pounds per year, 76 percent of which was transported to Lake Eucha by runoff. Spavinaw Creek transported about nine times more nitrogen load during base flow and about three times more nitrogen load during runoff to the lake than did Beaty Creek. Spavinaw Creek and Beaty Creek contributed an estimated mean annual phosphorus total load of 108,390 pounds per year, 91 percent of which was transported to Lake Eucha by runoff. Spavinaw Creek transported about 10 times more phosphorus load during base flow and about 2 times more phosphorus load during runoff to the lake than Beaty Creek. Nutrient loads at these stations do not represent the entire nutrient load to Lake Eucha, but the drainage area upstream from these stations accounts for about 62 percent of the drainage basin upstream from the lake.

Acknowledgments

The authors thank many people for their contributions to the data collection and data analysis presented in this report. Numerous City of Tulsa personnel participated in monthly water-quality sampling, and numerous USGS personnel participated in the runoff water-quality sampling. Special thanks goes to the USGS Tulsa Field Office for their contribution to the data collection. Additional thanks go to Dave Lorenz for help in the use of the load-estimation program, S-LOADEST; and Dave Mueller for insight into load-estimation equations.

References Cited

Akaike, Hirotugu, 1974, A new look at the statistical model identification: Institute of Electrical and Electronics Engineers, Transactions on Automatic Control, v. 19, no. 6, p. 716–723.

Adamski, J.C., Petersen, J.C., Freiwald, D.A., and Davis, J.V., 1995, Environmental and hydrologic setting of the Ozark Plateaus study unit, Arkansas, Kansas, Missouri, and Oklahoma: U.S. Geological Survey Water-Resources Investigations Report 94–4022, 69 p.

Blazs, R.L., Walters, D.M., Coffey, T.E., Boyle, D.L., and Wellman, J.J., 2003, Water resources data, Oklahoma, water year 2002: U.S. Geological Survey Water-Data Report OK–02–1, 375 p.

Blazs, R.L., Walters, D.M., Coffey, T.E., Boyle, D.L., and Wellman, J.J., 2004, Water resources data, Oklahoma, water year 2003: U.S. Geological Survey Water-Data Report OK–03–1, 394 p.

Blazs, R.L., Walters, D.M., Coffey, T.E., Boyle, D.L., and Wellman, J.J., 2005, Water resources data, Oklahoma, water year 2004: U.S. Geological Survey Water-Data Report OK–04–1, 408 p.

Blazs, R.L., Walters, D.M., Coffey, T.E., Boyle, D.L., and Wellman, J.J., 2006, Water resources data, Oklahoma, water year 2005: U.S. Geological Survey Water-Data Report OK–05–1, 473 p.

Childress, C.J.O., Foreman, W.T., Connor, B.F., and Maloney, T.J., 1999, New reporting procedures based on long-term method detection levels and some considerations for interpretations of water-quality data provided by the U.S. Geological Survey National Water Quality Laboratory: U.S. Geological Survey Open-File Report 99–193, 19 p.

Christensen, V.G., Esralew, R.A., and Allen, M.L., 2008, Estimated nutrient concentrations and continuous water-quality monitoring in the Eucha-Spavinaw Basin, northwestern Arkansas and northeastern Oklahoma, 2004–2007: U.S. Geological Survey Scientific Investigations Report 2008–5218, 32 p.

City of Tulsa City Services, 2008a, Water supply lakes—Eucha and Spavinaw watersheds, available only online at *http://www.cityoftulsa.org/CityServices/Water/EuchaSpavinaw.asp.* (Accessed June, 2008.)

City of Tulsa City Services, 2008b, Water treatment–History, available only online at *http://www.cityoftulsa.org/CityServices/Water/TreatmentHistory.asp.* (Accessed June, 2008.)

City of Tulsa City Services, 2008c, Water treatment process, available only online at *http://www.cityoftulsa.org/CityServices/Water/TreatmentProcess.asp.* (Accessed June, 2008.)

City of Tulsa, 2010, City of Tulsa's comprehensive watershed management approach: City of Tulsa Office of Water memorandum, 6 p.

Clark, G.M., Mueller, D.K., and Mast, M.A., 2000, Nutrient concentrations and yields in undeveloped stream basins of the United States: Journal of the American Water Resources Association, v. 36, no. 4, p. 849–860.

Cobb, E.D., and Biesecker, J.E., 1971, The National Hydrologic Benchmark Network: U.S. Geological Survey Circular 460–D, 38 p.

Cohn, T.A., 1988, Adjusted maximum likelihood estimation of the moments of lognormal populations from type I censored samples: U.S. Geological Survey Open-File Report 88–350, 34 p.

Cohn, T.A., DeLong, L.L., Gilroy, E.J., Hirsch, R.M., and Wells, D.K., 1989, Estimating constituent loads: Water Resources Research, v. 25, no. 5, p. 937–942.

Cohn, T.A., Gilroy, E.J., and Baier, W.G., 1992, Estimating fluvial transport of trace constituents using a regression model with data subject to censoring: Proceedings of the Joint Statistical Meeting, Boston, August 9–13, 1992, p. 142–151.

Cooke, G.W., and Williams, R.J.B, 1970, Losses of nitrogen and phosphorus from agricultural land: Journal of the Society for Water Treatment and Examination, v. 19, part 3, p. 253–276.

Crawford, C.G., 1991, Estimation of suspended-sediment rating curves and mean suspended-sediment loads: Journal of Hydrology, v. 129, p. 331–348.

Daniel, T.C., Sharpley, A.N., and Lemunyon, J.L., 1998, Agricultural phosphorus and eutrophication—A symposium overview: Journal of Environmental Quality, v. 27, no. 2, p. 251–257.

DeLaune, P.B., Haggard, B.E., Daniel, T.C., Chaubey, Indrajeet, and Cochran, M.J., 2006, The Eucha/Spavinaw phosphorus index—A court mandated index for litter management: Journal of Soil and Water Conservation, v. 61, no. 2, p. 1–10.

Dempster, A.P., Laird, N.M., and Rubin, D.B., 1977, Maximum likelihood from incomplete data via the EM algorithm: Journal of the Royal Statistical Society, Series B, v. 39, no. 1, p. 1–38.

Edwards, T.K., and Glysson, G.D., 1999, Field methods for measurement of fluvial sediment: U.S. Geological Survey Techniques of Water-Resources Investigations, book 3, chap. C2, 89 p.

Fenneman, N.M., 1938, Physiography of eastern United States: New York, McGraw-Hill, p. 631–662.

Gilliom, R.J., Alley, W.M., and Gurtz, M.E., 1995, Design of the National Water-Quality Assessment Program—Occurrence and distribution of water-quality conditions: U.S. Geological Survey Circular 1112, 33 p.

Gilliom, R.J., Hamilton, P.A., and Miller, T.L., 2001, The National Water-Quality Assessment Program—Entering a new decade of investigation: U.S. Geological Survey Fact Sheet 071–01, 6 p.

Haggard, B.E., 2000, Stream nutrient retention in the Lake Eucha-Spavinaw Basin: Stillwater, Okla., Oklahoma State University, Ph.D. Dissertation, 165 p.

Haggard, B.E., Storm, D.E., and Stanley, E.H., 2001, Effect of a point source input on stream nutrient retention: Journal of the American Water Resources Association, v. 37, no. 5, p. 1,291–1,299.

Helsel, D.R., and Hirsch, R.M., 1992, Statistical methods in water resources: Amsterdam, Netherlands, Elsevier, 522 p.

Institute of Hydrology, 1980a, Low flow studies: Wallingford, Oxon, United Kingdom, Report No. 1, 41 p.

Institute of Hydrology, 1980b, Low flow studies: Wallingford, Oxon, United Kingdom, Report No. 3, p. 12–19.

Jones, J.R., and Knowlton, M.F., 1993, Limnology of Missouri reservoirs: An analysis of regional patterns: Lake and Reservoir Management, v. 8, p. 17–30.

Langbein, W.B., and Iseri, K.T., 1960, General introductions and hydrologic definitions—Manual of Hydrology—Part 1, general surface-water techniques: U.S. Geological Survey Water-Supply Paper 1541–A, 29 p.

Levich, A.P., 1996, The role of nitrogen-phosphorus ratio in selecting for dominance of phytoplankton by cyanobacteria or green algae and its application to reservoir management: Journal of Aquatic Ecosystem Health, v. 5, no. 1, p. 55–61.

Mast, M.A., and Turk, J.T., 1999, Environmental characteristics and water quality of Hydrologic Benchmark Network Stations in the midwestern United States, 1963–95: U.S. Geological Survey Circular 1173–B, 130 p.

Multi-Resolution Land Characteristics Consortium, 2008, 2001 National Land Cover Database (NLCD), available online at *http://www.epa.gov/mrlc/nlcd-2001.html* (Accessed August, 2008.)

Oklahoma Water Resources Board, 2002, Water quality evaluation of the Eucha/Spavinaw Lake system, 528 p.

Petersen, J.C., Adamski, J.C., Bell, R.W., Davis, J.V., Femmer, S.R., Freiwald, D.A., and Joseph, R.L., 1998, Water quality in the Ozark Plateaus, Arkansas, Kansas, Missouri, and Oklahoma, 1992–1995: U.S. Geological Survey Circular 1158, available only online at *http://water.usgs.gov/pubs/circ/circ1158.*) (Accessed July, 2003.)

Rantz, S.E., and others, 1982, Measurement and computation of streamflow—Volume 2, computation of discharge: U.S. Geological Survey Water-Supply Paper 2175, v. 2, 285–631 p.

Runkel, R.L., Crawford, C.G., and Cohn, T.A., 2004, Load Estimator (LOADEST)—A FORTRAN program for estimating constituent loads in streams and rivers: U.S. Geological Survey Techniques and Methods, book 4, chap. A5, 69 p., available only online at *http://pubs.usgs.gov/tm/2005/tm4A5/*. (Accessed October, 2005.)

Sharpley, A.N., 1995, Fate and transport of nutrients—Phosphorus: U.S. Department of Agriculture, Agricultural Research Service Working Paper No. 8, 28 p.

Storm, D.E., White, Michael, Smolen, M.D., and Zhang, Hailin, 2001, Modeling phosphorus loading for the Lake Eucha Basin: Stillwater, Okla., Oklahoma State University, Biosystems and Agricultural Engineering Department, 14 p.

Storm, D.E., White, M.J., and Smolen, M.D., 2002, Modeling the Lake Eucha Basin using SWAT 2000: Stillwater, Okla., Oklahoma State University, Biosystems and Agricultural Engineering Department, 60 p.

TIBCO Software Incorporated, 2008, TIBCO Spotfire S-Plus Version 8.1.1 for Microsoft Windows professional developer edition with release 4.0 of the U.S. Geological Survey S-PLUS library: Palo Alto, California.

Tortorelli, R.L., 2006, Nutrient concentrations, loads, and yields in the Eucha-Spavinaw Basin, Arkansas and Oklahoma, 2002–2004: U.S. Geological Survey Scientific Investigations Report 2006–5250, 44 p.

Tortorelli, R.L., and Pickup, B.E., 2006, Phosphorus concentrations, loads, and yields in the Illinois River Basin, Arkansas and Oklahoma, 2000–2004: U.S. Geological Survey Scientific Investigations Report 2006–5175, 38 p.

Tortorelli, R.L., 2008, Nutrient concentrations, loads, and yields in the Eucha-Spavinaw Basin, Arkansas and Oklahoma, 2002–2006: U.S. Geological Survey Scientific Investigations Report 2008–5174, 56 p.

Tulsa Metropolitan Utility Authority, 2001, Eucha/Spavinaw watershed project: available only online at *http:www.tulsawater.com/eucha.html*. (Accessed August, 2006.)

United Nations Environmental Programme, 2007, Planning and management of lakes and reservoirs: an integrated approach to eutrophication, abridged version—a student's guide, available online at *http://www.unep.or.jp/ietc/Publications/TechPublications/TechPub-12/1-5.asp*. (Accessed July 11, 2007).

U.S. Department of Agriculture, 2004, The census of agriculture: 2002 census report, available online at *http://www.agcensus.usda.gov/Publications/2002/index.asp*. (Accessed April, 2010.)

U.S. Department of Agriculture, 2009, The census of agriculture: 2007 census report, available online at *http://www.agcensus.usda.gov/Publications/2007/Full_Report/index.asp*. (Accessed April, 2010.)

U.S. Environmental Protection Agency, 1983, Methods for chemical analysis of water and wastes, Method 365.2 (2nd ed.): EPA-600/4-79-20 Revised March 1983 [variously paged].

U.S. Environmental Protection Agency, 1993, Methods for the determination of inorganic substances in environmental samples: EPA-600/R-93-100 [variously paged].

U.S. Environmental Protection Agency Region 6 and Oklahoma Department of Environmental Quality, 2009, TMDL development for Lakes Eucha and Spavinaw in Oklahoma, 36 p., available online at *http://www.deq.state.ok.us/wqdnew/tmdl/eucha_spavinaw/eucha_lk_spavinaw_%20ck_%20final_tmdl_2009-09-01.pdf*. (Accessed March, 2010.)

U.S. Geological Survey, 1999, The quality of our Nation's waters—Nutrients and Pesticides: U.S. Geological Survey Circular 1225, 82 p.

U.S. Geological Survey, 2006, National field manual for the collection of water-quality data, collection of water samples: U.S. Geological Survey Techniques of Water-Resources Investigations, book 9, chap. A4, 166 p., available online at *http://water.usgs.gov/owq/FieldManual/chapter4/pdf/Chap4_v2.pdf*. (Accessed September, 2008.)

U.S. Geological Survey, 2007, Water-resources data for the United States, water year 2006, available only online at *http://wdr.water.usgs.gov/wy2006/search.jsp*. (Accessed January, 2008.)

U.S. Geological Survey, 2008a, National Hydrography Dataset: U.S. Geological Survey, available only online at *http://nhd.usgs.gov*. (Accessed April, 2010.).

U.S. Geological Survey, 2008b, Water-resources data for the United States, water year 2007: available only online at *http://wdr.water.usgs.gov/wy2007/search.jsp*. (Accessed April, 2008.)

U.S. Geological Survey, 2009, Water-resources data for the United States, water year 2008: available only online at, accessed April 10, 2009, at *http://wdr.water.usgs.gov/wy2007/search.jsp*. (Accessed April, 2009.)

U.S. Geological Survey, 2010, Water-resources data for the United States, water year 2009: (online only), available only online at *http://wdr.water.usgs.gov/wy2007/search.jsp*. (Accessed March, 2010.)

Wagner, Kevin, and Woodruff, Scott, 1997, Phase I clean lakes project, diagnostic and feasibility study of Lake Eucha: Oklahoma Conservation Commission, Final Report.

Wahl, K.L., and Tortorelli, R.L., 1997, Changes in flow in the Beaver-North Canadian River Basin upstream from Canton Lake, western Oklahoma: U.S. Geological Survey Water-Resources Investigations Report 96–4304, 58 p.

Wahl, K.L., and Wahl, T.L., 1995, Determining the flow of Comal Springs at New Braunfels, Texas, *in* Proceedings of Texas water, '95, A Component Conference of the First International Conference on Water Resources Engineering, American Society of Civil Engineers Symposium, San Antonio, Texas, August 16–17, 1995: American Society of Civil Engineers, p. 77–86.

Wolynetz, M.S., 1979, Algorithm 139–Maximum likelihood estimation in a linear model with confined and censored data: Applied Statistics, v. 28, p. 195–206.

Appendixes 1–5

Appendix 1. Streamflows, and total nitrogen and total phosphorus concentrations for Spavinaw Creek near Maysville, Arkansas, 2002–09.

[COT, City of Tulsa; USGS, U.S. Geological Survey; ft³/s, cubic foot per second; mg/L, milligram per liter; N, nitrogen; P, phosphorus; --, not reported; all water-quality and streamflow data available at *http://water.usgs.gov/ok/nwis*]

Date	Sample time	Agency collecting sample	Streamflow[1] (ft³/s)	Total nitrogen concentration (mg/L as N)[2]	Total phosphorus concentration (mg/L as P)	Flow category[3]
1/15/2002	0820	COT	35	4.80	0.03	Base flow
2/1/2002	1010	USGS	305	3.40	.05	Runoff
2/12/2002	0815	COT	55	4.80	.02	Base flow
3/12/2002	0845	COT	61	4.20	.02	Base flow
3/20/2002	1445	USGS	221	4.00	.03	Runoff
4/8/2002	1205	USGS	648	3.97	.16	Runoff
4/18/2002	0817	COT	82	4.20	.03	Base flow
5/13/2002	1320	USGS	176	3.44	.03	Runoff
5/17/2002	1300	USGS	1,560	7.40	.50	Runoff
5/23/2002	0808	COT	136	4.54	.04	Runoff
6/13/2002	0838	COT	88	3.68	.04	Runoff
7/18/2002	0832	COT	34	3.41	.03	Base flow
8/13/2002	0820	COT	24	3.20	.03	Base flow
9/19/2002	0810	COT	19	2.85	.03	Base flow
10/16/2002	0735	COT	16	2.80	.03	Base flow
11/12/2002	0753	COT	18	2.85	.03	Base flow
12/12/2002	0818	COT	17	2.90	.02	Base flow
1/7/2003	0845	COT	25	3.36	.02	Base flow
2/6/2003	0817	COT	18	3.15	.02	Base flow
3/5/2003	0818	COT	62	4.43	.03	Runoff
4/9/2003	0822	COT	38	3.76	.02	Base flow
5/8/2003	0825	COT	29	3.10	.02	Base flow
5/16/2003	1100	USGS	92	3.63	.22	Runoff
5/20/2003	1102	USGS	153	3.70	.06	Runoff
5/21/2003	1115	USGS	251	4.16	.04	Runoff
6/2/2003	1258	USGS	49	4.20	.04	Runoff
6/3/2003	0830	COT	48	3.85	--	Runoff
6/12/2003	1102	USGS	48	3.82	.20	Runoff
7/10/2003	0800	COT	21	3.33	.02	Base flow
7/14/2003	1235	USGS	69	3.01	.04	Runoff
8/5/2003	0800	COT	15	2.97	.03	Base flow
9/11/2003	0759	COT	14	2.70	.03	Base flow
10/9/2003	0755	COT	14	2.57	.04	Base flow
11/6/2003	0755	COT	13	2.60	.02	Base flow
11/19/2003	1111	USGS	33	3.06	.03	Runoff
12/10/2003	0820	COT	21	3.53	.02	Base flow
1/6/2004	0840	COT	59	4.28	.02	Runoff
2/5/2004	0815	COT	38	4.55	.02	Base flow
3/4/2004	0825	COT	890	5.57	.29	Runoff
3/4/2004	1125	USGS	809	5.79	.14	Runoff
3/29/2004	1110	USGS	307	4.40	.05	Runoff
4/7/2004	0845	COT	72	4.86	.02	Base flow
4/23/2004	1040	USGS	419	3.43	.05	Runoff
4/24/2004	1435	USGS	2,110	5.68	.80	Runoff

Appendix 1.   Streamflows, and total nitrogen and total phosphorus concentrations for Spavinaw Creek near Maysville, Arkansas, 2002–09.—Continued

[COT, City of Tulsa; USGS, U.S. Geological Survey; ft³/s, cubic foot per second; mg/L, milligram per liter; N, nitrogen; P, phosphorus; --, not reported; all water-quality and streamflow data available at *http://water.usgs.gov/ok/nwis*]

Date	Sample time	Agency collecting sample	Streamflow[1] (ft³/s)	Total nitrogen concentration (mg/L as N)[2]	Total phosphorus concentration (mg/L as P)	Flow category[3]
5/6/2004	0817	COT	160	4.87	0.03	Runoff
6/10/2004	0815	COT	43	3.82	.04	Base flow
7/3/2004	1100	USGS	3,970	5.61	.92	Runoff
7/8/2004	0830	COT	170	4.61	.02	Runoff
8/5/2004	0825	COT	64	3.91	.04	Base flow
9/9/2004	0830	COT	29	3.59	.03	Base flow
10/7/2004	0806	COT	22	3.37	.03	Base flow
11/1/2004	1200	USGS	654	4.02	.24	Runoff
11/3/2004	0848	COT	156	4.67	.05	Runoff
12/9/2004	0840	COT	151	5.18	.03	Runoff
1/5/2005	1215	USGS	3,190	9.34	1.2	Runoff
1/6/2005	0858	COT	855	5.57	.17	Runoff
2/10/2005	0832	COT	84	4.80	.03	Base flow
3/10/2005	0837	COT	72	4.36	.03	Base flow
4/7/2005	0845	COT	167	3.88	.06	Runoff
5/12/2005	0825	COT	41	3.87	.03	Base flow
6/9/2005	0902	COT	33	3.53	.03	Base flow
6/14/2005	1145	USGS	78	3.50	.15	Runoff
7/14/2005	0827	COT	22	2.90	.03	Base flow
8/11/2005	0757	COT	19	2.82	.03	Base flow
9/15/2005	0835	COT	15	2.70	.06	Base flow
10/6/2005	0815	COT	13	2.75	.04	Base flow
11/16/2005	0752	COT	16	2.73	.03	Base flow
12/15/2005	0812	COT	14	2.82	.02	Base flow
1/12/2006	0812	COT	16	2.82	.12	Base flow
2/9/2006	0823	COT	14	2.73	.03	Base flow
3/9/2006	0805	COT	14	2.60	.02	Base flow
4/12/2006	0802	COT	18	2.66	--	Base flow
4/29/2006	1330	USGS	29	2.37	.03	Runoff
5/2/2006	1335	USGS	84	3.22	.03	Runoff
5/10/2006	0830	COT	63	.69	.05	Runoff
5/10/2006	1135	USGS	61	3.15	.04	Runoff
6/8/2006	0837	COT	28	--[4]	.03	Runoff
7/13/2006	0856	COT	9.8	--[4]	.04	Base flow
7/13/2006	1100	USGS	9.8	2.37	.03	Base flow
8/10/2006	0755	COT	6.0	1.98	--	Base flow
8/28/2006	1135	USGS	61	2.29	.06	Runoff
9/14/2006	0837	COT	12	2.71	--	Base flow
10/12/2006	0837	COT	11	2.85	--	Base flow
11/16/2006	0730	COT	16	2.39	--	Base flow
12/6/2006	0847	COT	70	5.00	--	Runoff
1/11/2007	0908	COT	38	6.00	.07	Base flow
1/23/2007	1100	USGS	145	5.64	.04	Runoff
2/8/2007	0855	COT	39	5.20	.02	Base flow

Appendix 1. Streamflows, and total nitrogen and total phosphorus concentrations for Spavinaw Creek near Maysville, Arkansas, 2002–09.—Continued

[COT, City of Tulsa; USGS, U.S. Geological Survey; ft³/s, cubic foot per second; mg/L, milligram per liter; N, nitrogen; P, phosphorus; --, not reported; all water-quality and streamflow data available at *http://water.usgs.gov/ok/nwis*]

Date	Sample time	Agency collecting sample	Streamflow[1] (ft³/s)	Total nitrogen concentration (mg/L as N)[2]	Total phosphorus concentration (mg/L as P)	Flow category[3]
3/7/2007	0857	COT	41	4.74	0.03	Base flow
4/19/2007	0850	COT	40	3.43	.03	Runoff
5/8/2007	0827	COT	72	2.87	.04	Runoff
5/8/2007	1330	USGS	73	3.10	.04	Runoff
5/30/2007	1045	USGS	26	3.09	.03	Base flow
6/7/2007	0822	COT	23	3.00	.03	Base flow
6/20/2007	1330	USGS	22	2.86	.03	Base flow
7/12/2007	0829	COT	19	2.63	.03	Base flow
7/25/2007	1130	USGS	17	2.53	.07	Base flow
8/9/2007	0600	COT	12	2.50	.04	Base flow
9/7/2007	1230	USGS	67	2.71	.04	Runoff
9/13/2007	0840	COT	49	3.82	.02	Runoff
10/3/2007	1215	USGS	232	4.30	.11	Runoff
10/3/2007	1215	USGS	235	4.30	.11	Runoff
10/11/2007	0845	COT	45	4.70	.03	Runoff
11/8/2007	0805	COT	23	4.30	.03	Base flow
12/12/2007	1125	USGS	271	6.20	.05	Runoff
12/18/2007	1213	COT	147	5.90	.03	Runoff
1/8/2008	1100	USGS	1,960	7.27	.70	Runoff
1/17/2008	0910	COT	82	6.10	.04	Runoff
2/14/2008	0850	COT	88	4.90	.03	Runoff
2/17/2008	1420	USGS	1,420	5.58	.52	Runoff
3/3/2008	1100	USGS	764	4.26	.11	Runoff
3/12/2008	0850	COT	112	5.40	--	Base flow
3/18/2008	1115	USGS	3,170	5.69	.94	Runoff
4/16/2008	0850	COT	215	4.48	.04	Base flow
5/7/2008	0845	COT	120	4.00	.03	Base flow
6/12/2008	0900	COT	251	3.80	.05	Runoff
7/16/2008	0840	COT	145	4.00	.04	Runoff
8/14/2008	0900	COT	66	3.70	.04	Base flow
9/5/2008	1100	USGS	198	3.60	.05	Runoff
9/11/2008	0845	COT	67	3.90	.04	Base flow
9/14/2008	1045	USGS	789	4.05	.36	Runoff
10/9/2008	0940	COT	49	4.10	.03	Base flow
11/6/2008	0840	COT	42	3.80	.04	Base flow
12/11/2008	0915	COT	29	4.00	.04	Base flow
1/8/2009	0925	COT	31	3.90	.03	Base flow
2/12/2009	0900	COT	427	4.30	.05	Runoff
2/12/2009	1030	USGS	416	4.50	.05	Runoff
3/5/2009	0820	COT	45	4.40	.04	Base flow
4/16/2009	0850	COT	208	4.10	.09	Runoff
5/4/2009	1030	USGS	730	3.30	.07	Runoff
5/8/2009	1350	USGS	1,515	3.15	.68	Runoff
5/14/2009	0855	COT	330	4.20	.27	Runoff

Appendix 1.   Streamflows, and total nitrogen and total phosphorus concentrations for Spavinaw Creek near Maysville, Arkansas, 2002–09.—Continued

[COT, City of Tulsa; USGS, U.S. Geological Survey; ft³/s, cubic foot per second; mg/L, milligram per liter; N, nitrogen; P, phosphorus; --, not reported; all water-quality and streamflow data available at *http://water.usgs.gov/ok/nwis*]

Date	Sample time	Agency collecting sample	Streamflow[1] (ft³/s)	Total nitrogen concentration (mg/L as N)[2]	Total phosphorus concentration (mg/L as P)	Flow category[3]
6/11/2009	0855	COT	115	4.00	0.04	Runoff
7/9/2009	0840	COT	43	3.80	.04	Base flow
8/13/2009	0900	COT	51	3.60	.04	Runoff
9/10/2009	0850	COT	47	3.58	.05	Runoff
10/8/2009	0745	COT	34	3.70	.03	Base flow
10/9/2009	1015	USGS	3,580	5.43	.90	Runoff
11/5/2009	0840	COT	119	4.50	.04	Runoff
12/9/2009	0850	COT	57	4.20	.03	Base flow

[1] Streamflow for data collected by USGS is measured instantaneous streamflow; streamflow for data collected by COT is daily mean streamflow unless streamflow changing rapidly during the day, then it is 15-minute unit value.

[2] Total nitrogen is calculated by adding Kjeldahl-N and nitrite plus nitrate analyses.

[3] Base flow and runoff designated by Base-Flow Index (BFI) program (Institute of Hydrology, 1980a, 1980b).

[4] Nitrite plus nitrate analyses not reported, nitrate analyses were substituted in the total nitrogen calculation for this sample.

Appendix 2. Streamflows, and total nitrogen and total phosphorus concentrations for Spavinaw Creek near Cherokee, Arkansas, 2002–09.

[COT, City of Tulsa; USGS, U.S. Geological Survey; ft³/s, cubic foot per second; mg/L, milligram per liter; N, nitrogen; P, phosphorus; --, not reported; all water-quality and streamflow data available at *http://water.usgs.gov/ok/nwis*]

Date	Sample time	Agency collecting sample	Streamflow[1] (ft³/s)	Total nitrogen concentration (mg/L as N)[2]	Total phosphorus concentration (mg/L as P)	Flow category[3]
1/15/2002	0835	COT	41	5.40	0.23	Base flow
2/1/2002	1236	USGS	290	3.60	.17	Runoff
2/12/2002	0835	COT	71	5.20	.23	Base flow
3/12/2002	0900	COT	82	4.40	.23	Base flow
3/20/2002	1641	USGS	233	4.83	.17	Runoff
4/8/2002	1410	USGS	700	4.26	.19	Runoff
4/18/2002	0835	COT	101	4.60	.20	Base flow
5/13/2002	1510	USGS	190	3.28	.17	Runoff
5/17/2002	1630	USGS	1,590	6.82	.38	Runoff
5/23/2002	0823	COT	150	4.40	.17	Runoff
6/13/2002	0850	COT	107	3.92	.19	Runoff
7/18/2002	0847	COT	42	3.59	.23	Base flow
8/13/2002	0835	COT	26	3.33	.23	Base flow
9/19/2002	0825	COT	25	3.16	.30	Base flow
10/16/2002	0755	COT	17	3.11	.32	Base flow
11/12/2002	0808	COT	24	3.49	.31	Base flow
12/12/2002	0833	COT	19	3.54	.30	Base flow
1/7/2003	0900	COT	33	4.11	.30	Runoff
2/6/2003	0834	COT	20	4.13	.26	Base flow
3/5/2003	0900	COT	67	4.94	.19	Runoff
4/9/2003	0836	COT	54	4.22	.18	Base flow
5/8/2003	0840	COT	32	3.28	.23	Base flow
5/14/2003	0800	COT	31	4.44	.22	Base flow
5/16/2003	0945	COT	134	3.05	.50	Runoff
5/16/2003	1211	USGS	134	3.21	.03	Runoff
5/20/2003	1258	USGS	165	4.00	.25	Runoff
5/21/2003	1247	USGS	310	4.34	.13	Runoff
6/2/2003	1405	USGS	54	2.48	.19	Runoff
6/3/2003	0850	COT	52	4.27	.14	Runoff
6/11/2003	0910	COT	38	4.10	.19	Base flow
6/12/2003	1218	USGS	49	4.20	.03	Runoff
7/10/2003	0815	COT	22	3.64	.20	Base flow
7/14/2003	1054	USGS	61	3.46	.17	Runoff
8/5/2003	0820	COT	17	3.45	.21	Base flow
9/11/2003	0826	COT	16	3.51	.21	Base flow
10/9/2003	0815	COT	21	3.66	.22	Base flow
11/6/2003	0811	COT	19	3.90	.23	Base flow
11/19/2003	1236	USGS	41	4.22	.23	Runoff
12/10/2003	0845	COT	29	4.21	.18	Runoff
1/6/2004	0855	COT	79	4.99	.15	Runoff
2/5/2004	0835	COT	49	5.46	.14	Base flow
3/4/2004	0840	COT	1,100	5.73	.34	Runoff
3/4/2004	1510	USGS	912	6.28	.20	Runoff
3/29/2004	1235	USGS	375	4.52	.10	Runoff

Appendix 2. Streamflows, and total nitrogen and total phosphorus concentrations for Spavinaw Creek near Cherokee, Arkansas, 2002–09.—Continued

[COT, City of Tulsa; USGS, U.S. Geological Survey; ft³/s, cubic foot per second; mg/L, milligram per liter; N, nitrogen; P, phosphorus; --, not reported; all water-quality and streamflow data available at *http://water.usgs.gov/ok/nwis*]

Date	Sample time	Agency collecting sample	Streamflow[1] (ft³/s)	Total nitrogen concentration (mg/L as N)[2]	Total phosphorus concentration (mg/L as P)	Flow category[3]
4/7/2004	0900	COT	80	5.12	0.11	Base flow
4/23/2004	1259	USGS	470	3.87	.08	Runoff
4/24/2004	1735	USGS	2,210	4.99	.64	Runoff
5/6/2004	0837	COT	207	5.22	.11	Runoff
6/10/2004	0830	COT	57	4.21	.14	Base flow
7/3/2004	0926	USGS	8,000	2.68	1.30	Runoff
7/8/2004	0845	COT	207	5.04	.13	Runoff
8/5/2004	0840	COT	86	4.48	.19	Base flow
9/9/2004	0845	COT	33	4.20	.14	Base flow
10/7/2004	0820	COT	24	4.30	.16	Base flow
11/1/2004	1400	USGS	657	4.66	.24	Runoff
11/3/2004	0905	COT	199	5.20	.15	Runoff
12/9/2004	0855	COT	184	5.58	.11	Runoff
1/5/2005	1325	USGS	3,780	10.4	1.20	Runoff
1/6/2005	0915	COT	1,440	6.13	.23	Runoff
2/10/2005	0848	COT	97	5.30	.08	Base flow
3/10/2005	0852	COT	83	4.89	.09	Base flow
4/7/2005	0900	COT	219	4.18	.19	Runoff
5/12/2005	0840	COT	37	4.13	.15	Base flow
6/9/2005	0919	COT	35	3.81	.11	Base flow
6/14/2005	1440	USGS	105	3.34	.14	Runoff
7/14/2005	0844	COT	24	3.28	.17	Base flow
8/11/2005	0815	COT	22	3.99	.16	Base flow
10/6/2005	0825	COT	16	3.55	.16	Base flow
11/16/2005	0815	COT	25	4.04	.15	Base flow
12/15/2005	0828	COT	14	3.69	.12	Base flow
1/12/2006	0825	COT	18	4.37	.14	Base flow
2/9/2006	0840	COT	16	3.98	.16	Base flow
3/9/2006	0820	COT	19	3.71	.12	Base flow
4/12/2006	0818	COT	26	2.96	--	Runoff
4/29/2006	1645	USGS	46	3.15	.15	Runoff
5/2/2006	1455	USGS	103	3.51	.13	Runoff
5/10/2006	0845	COT	112	3.37	.14	Runoff
5/10/2006	1245	USGS	101	3.67	.13	Runoff
6/8/2006	0853	COT	29	--[4]	.15	Runoff
7/13/2006	0920	COT	13	--[4]	.15	Base flow
7/13/2006	1245	USGS	13	2.97	.13	Base flow
8/10/2006	0810	COT	10	2.56	--	Base flow
8/28/2006	1315	USGS	77	4.28	.19	Runoff
9/14/2006	0855	COT	16	3.72	--	Base flow
10/12/2006	0857	COT	15	3.68	--	Base flow
11/16/2006	0745	COT	26	3.34	--	Runoff
12/6/2006	0905	COT	80	5.57	--	Runoff
1/11/2007	0930	COT	40	5.74	.09	Base flow

Appendix 2.   Streamflows, and total nitrogen and total phosphorus concentrations for Spavinaw Creek near Cherokee, Arkansas, 2002–09.—Continued

[COT, City of Tulsa; USGS, U.S. Geological Survey; ft³/s, cubic foot per second; mg/L, milligram per liter; N, nitrogen; P, phosphorus; --, not reported; all water-quality and streamflow data available at *http://water.usgs.gov/ok/nwis*]

Date	Sample time	Agency collecting sample	Streamflow[1] (ft³/s)	Total nitrogen concentration (mg/L as N)[2]	Total phosphorus concentration (mg/L as P)	Flow category[3]
1/23/2007	1400	USGS	187	6.04	0.09	Runoff
2/8/2007	0912	COT	52	6.08	.09	Base flow
3/7/2007	0912	COT	47	5.07	.09	Base flow
4/19/2007	0910	COT	54	3.73	.08	Runoff
5/8/2007	0845	COT	103	3.27	.09	Runoff
5/8/2007	1430	USGS	101	3.31	.09	Runoff
5/30/2007	1200	USGS	33	3.22	.10	Base flow
6/7/2007	0738	COT	29	3.26	.09	Base flow
6/20/2007	1145	USGS	27	3.20	.10	Base flow
7/12/2007	0845	COT	26	2.82	.10	Base flow
7/25/2007	1230	USGS	20	2.52	.10	Base flow
8/9/2007	0827	COT	15	2.45	.11	Base flow
9/7/2007	1345	USGS	77	2.85	.12	Runoff
9/13/2007	0900	COT	71	3.98	.09	Runoff
10/3/2007	1600	USGS	292	4.80	.16	Runoff
10/11/2007	0905	COT	77	5.40	.12	Runoff
10/18/2007	1405	USGS	75	4.60	.10	Runoff
11/8/2007	0822	COT	34	4.90	.10	Base flow
12/12/2007	1235	USGS	409	5.80	.08	Runoff
12/18/2007	1230	COT	143	6.70	.07	Runoff
1/8/2008	1330	USGS	2,370	7.14	.63	Runoff
1/17/2008	0928	COT	103	6.70	.09	Runoff
2/14/2008	0905	COT	117	5.30	.07	Runoff
2/17/2008	1530	USGS	1,950	6.04	.38	Runoff
3/3/2008	1345	USGS	832	4.32	.11	Runoff
3/12/2008	0915	COT	131	5.70	.06	Base flow
3/18/2008	1530	USGS	5,030	6.14	1.60	Runoff
4/16/2008	0905	COT	276	4.60	.08	Base flow
5/7/2008	0905	COT	125	4.20	.06	Base flow
6/12/2008	0920	COT	327	3.90	.10	Runoff
7/16/2008	0855	COT	184	4.20	.08	Runoff
8/14/2008	0920	COT	78	4.10	.09	Runoff
9/5/2008	1230	USGS	208	4.09	.09	Runoff
9/11/2008	0900	COT	87	4.40	.08	Base flow
9/14/2008	1200	USGS	923	4.33	.18	Runoff
10/9/2008	0925	COT	60	4.60	.08	Base flow
11/6/2008	0900	COT	46	4.40	.07	Base flow
12/11/2008	0935	COT	35	4.30	.08	Base flow
1/8/2009	0945	COT	38	4.60	.07	Base flow
2/12/2009	0915	COT	366	4.80	.07	Runoff
2/12/2009	1115	USGS	358	4.60	.07	Runoff
3/5/2009	0838	COT	54	4.80	.07	Base flow
4/16/2009	0910	COT	251	4.50	.07	Runoff
5/4/2009	1145	USGS	626	3.80	.07	Runoff

Appendix 2.   Streamflows, and total nitrogen and total phosphorus concentrations for Spavinaw Creek near Cherokee, Arkansas, 2002–09.—Continued

[COT, City of Tulsa; USGS, U.S. Geological Survey; ft³/s, cubic foot per second; mg/L, milligram per liter; N, nitrogen; P, phosphorus; --, not reported; all water-quality and streamflow data available at *http://water.usgs.gov/ok/nwis*]

Date	Sample time	Agency collecting sample	Streamflow[1] (ft³/s)	Total nitrogen concentration (mg/L as N)[2]	Total phosphorus concentration (mg/L as P)	Flow category[3]
5/8/2009	1330	USGS	1,030	6.40	0.43	Runoff
5/14/2009	0915	COT	273	5.24	.11	Runoff
6/11/2009	0915	COT	128	4.30	.09	Runoff
7/9/2009	0855	COT	46	4.20	.08	Base flow
8/13/2009	0920	COT	63	3.80	.09	Runoff
9/10/2009	0900	COT	58	3.40	.10	Runoff
10/8/2009	0800	COT	40	4.00	.10	Base flow
10/9/2009	1200	USGS	3,800	6.12	1.10	Runoff
11/5/2009	0900	COT	133	4.80	.09	Runoff
12/9/2009	0910	COT	62	4.50	.09	Base flow

[1] Streamflow for data collected by USGS is measured instantaneous streamflow; streamflow for data collected by COT is daily mean streamflow unless streamflow changing rapidly during the day, then it is 15-minute unit value.

[2] Total nitrogen is calculated by adding Kjeldahl-N and nitrite plus nitrate analyses.

[3] Base flow and runoff designated by Base-Flow Index (BFI) program (Institute of Hydrology, 1980a, 1980b).

[4] Nitrite plus nitrate analyses not reported, nitrate analyses were substituted in the total nitrogen calculation for this sample.

Appendix 3.   Streamflows, and total nitrogen and total phosphorus concentrations for Spavinaw Creek near Sycamore, Oklahoma, 2002–09.

[COT, City of Tulsa; USGS, U.S. Geological Survey; ft3/s, cubic foot per second; mg/L, milligram per liter; N, nitrogen; P, phosphorus; --, not reported; all water-quality and streamflow data available at *http://water.usgs.gov/ok/nwis*]

Date	Sample time	Agency collecting sample	Streamflow[1] (ft^3/s)	Total nitrogen concentration (mg/L as N)[2]	Total phosphorus concentration (mg/L as P)	Flow category[3]
1/15/2002	0755	COT	54	5.50	0.14	Base flow
2/1/2002	1506	USGS	384	3.20	.16	Runoff
2/12/2002	0750	COT	92	5.30	.15	Base flow
3/12/2002	0815	COT	105	4.50	.15	Base flow
3/21/2002	1123	USGS	268	4.40	.14	Runoff
4/8/2002	1708	USGS	952	5.06	.18	Runoff
4/18/2002	0817	COT	131	4.70	.15	Base flow
5/13/2002	1205	USGS	203	3.84	.17	Runoff
5/17/2002	1428	USGS	885	7.10	.31	Runoff
5/23/2002	0740	COT	174	4.30	.15	Runoff
6/13/2002	0803	COT	135	3.96	.15	Base flow
7/18/2002	0800	COT	46	3.65	.14	Base flow
1/7/2003	0818	COT	44	4.07	.16	Runoff
3/5/2003	0700	COT	110	4.97	.14	Runoff
4/9/2003	0757	COT	57	4.02	.14	Base flow
5/16/2003	1335	USGS	151	3.68	.19	Runoff
5/20/2003	1705	USGS	242	4.10	.27	Runoff
5/21/2003	1437	USGS	345	4.29	.10	Runoff
6/2/2003	1519	USGS	68	3.87	.13	Runoff
6/3/2003	0800	COT	71	4.25	--	Runoff
6/16/2003	1312	USGS	72	3.99	.13	Runoff
9/2/2003	1220	USGS	22	3.58	.17	Runoff
1/6/2004	0815	COT	93	5.38	.12	Runoff
1/18/2004	1540	USGS	137	5.70	.12	Runoff
2/5/2004	0740	COT	56	5.36	.11	Base flow
3/4/2004	0754	COT	1,500	6.15	.46	Runoff
3/4/2004	1135	USGS	1,310	6.44	.19	Runoff
3/29/2004	1430	USGS	462	4.82	.10	Runoff
4/7/2004	0817	COT	100	5.22	.09	Base flow
4/23/2004	1445	USGS	561	3.54	.12	Runoff
4/24/2004	1445	USGS	3,120	5.97	.97	Runoff
5/6/2004	0750	COT	291	5.17	.10	Runoff
6/10/2004	0750	COT	62	4.24	.13	Base flow
7/3/2004	1327	USGS	4,810	5.48	.98	Runoff
7/8/2004	0800	COT	330	5.05	.12	Runoff
8/5/2004	0755	COT	148	4.39	.12	Base flow
9/9/2004	0800	COT	50	4.21	.12	Base flow
11/1/2004	1600	USGS	1,010	4.95	.24	Runoff
11/3/2004	0818	COT	353	5.21	.15	Runoff
12/9/2004	0812	COT	317	5.58	.09	Runoff
1/5/2005	1440	USGS	3,860	9.36	1.2	Runoff
1/6/2005	0827	COT	1,690	5.89	.25	Runoff
2/10/2005	0805	COT	117	5.45	.10	Base flow
3/10/2005	0811	COT	100	4.88	.11	Base flow

Appendix 3.   Streamflows, and total nitrogen and total phosphorus concentrations for Spavinaw Creek near Sycamore, Oklahoma, 2002–09.—Continued

[COT, City of Tulsa; USGS, U.S. Geological Survey; ft3/s, cubic foot per second; mg/L, milligram per liter; N, nitrogen; P, phosphorus; --, not reported; all water-quality and streamflow data available at *http://water.usgs.gov/ok/nwis*]

Date	Sample time	Agency collecting sample	Streamflow[1] (ft³/s)	Total nitrogen concentration (mg/L as N)[2]	Total phosphorus concentration (mg/L as P)	Flow category[3]
4/7/2005	0815	COT	292	4.87	0.09	Runoff
5/12/2005	0755	COT	51	4.29	.14	Base flow
6/9/2005	0830	COT	41	3.92	.10	Base flow
6/15/2005	1115	USGS	89	3.85	.11	Runoff
4/29/2006	1845	USGS	27	3.15	.11	Runoff
5/2/2006	1515	USGS	109	3.83	.08	Runoff
5/10/2006	0803	COT	101	3.86	.13	Runoff
5/10/2006	1330	USGS	150	3.52	.13	Runoff
7/13/2006	0825	COT	5.8	--	.12	Base flow
7/13/2006	0900	USGS	5.8	3.18	.10	Base flow
8/28/2006	1145	USGS	18	3.03	.12	Runoff
12/6/2006	0814	COT	104	5.60	--	Runoff
1/11/2007	0837	COT	42	7.35	.18	Base flow
1/23/2007	1430	USGS	293	6.24	.08	Runoff
2/8/2007	0827	COT	58	5.90	.08	Base flow
3/7/2007	0825	COT	51	5.32	.09	Base flow
4/19/2007	0822	COT	65	4.03	.09	Runoff
5/8/2007	0755	COT	233	3.59	.10	Runoff
5/8/2007	1100	USGS	226	3.50	.08	Runoff
5/29/2007	1115	USGS	35	3.41	.08	Base flow
6/20/2007	1030	USGS	36	3.26	.09	Base flow
7/25/2007	0945	USGS	29	2.80	.08	Base flow
9/10/2007	1145	USGS	163	3.75	.10	Runoff
9/13/2007	0811	COT	83	3.83	.10	Runoff
10/3/2007	1400	USGS	663	5.20	.19	Runoff
10/11/2007	0810	COT	96	5.50	.09	Runoff
12/11/2007	1515	USGS	640	5.70	.09	Runoff
12/18/2007	1142	COT	214	6.60	.07	Runoff
1/8/2008	1305	USGS	3,040	7.67	.75	Runoff
1/17/2008	0835	COT	134	6.70	.10	Runoff
2/14/2008	0818	COT	143	5.50	.07	Runoff
2/17/2008	1245	USGS	2,320	5.91	.40	Runoff
3/3/2008	1215	USGS	1,200	4.93	.23	Runoff
3/12/2008	0817	COT	137	5.80	--	Base flow
3/18/2008	1130	USGS	5,280	5.84	.98	Runoff
4/16/2008	0810	COT	318	4.50	.08	Base flow
5/7/2008	0815	COT	150	4.38	.11	Base flow
6/12/2008	0824	COT	434	4.00	.10	Runoff
7/16/2008	0810	COT	266	4.20	.08	Runoff
8/14/2008	0825	COT	106	4.20	.08	Runoff
9/5/2008	1400	USGS	297	4.00	.09	Runoff
9/11/2008	0810	COT	119	4.30	.08	Base flow
9/14/2008	1320	USGS	1,210	4.36	.20	Runoff
10/9/2008	0840	COT	63	4.60	.08	Base flow

Appendix 3. Streamflows, and total nitrogen and total phosphorus concentrations for Spavinaw Creek near Sycamore, Oklahoma, 2002–09.—Continued

[COT, City of Tulsa; USGS, U.S. Geological Survey; ft3/s, cubic foot per second; mg/L, milligram per liter; N, nitrogen; P. phosphorus; --, not reported; all water-quality and streamflow data available at *http://water.usgs.gov/ok/nwis*]

Date	Sample time	Agency collecting sample	Streamflow[1] (ft³/s)	Total nitrogen concentration (mg/L as N)[2]	Total phosphorus concentration (mg/L as P)	Flow category[3]
11/6/2008	0810	COT	45	4.50	0.08	Base flow
12/11/2008	0845	COT	32	4.60	.09	Base flow
1/8/2009	0855	COT	45	4.60	.08	Base flow
2/11/2009	1345	USGS	249	4.80	.10	Runoff
2/12/2009	0830	COT	472	4.80	.08	Runoff
3/5/2009	0752	COT	58	5.00	.08	Base flow
4/16/2009	0815	COT	167	4.6	.10	Runoff
5/4/2009	1400	USGS	689	4.10	.07	Runoff
5/8/2009	1515	USGS	975	6.16	.42	Runoff
5/14/2009	0820	COT	358	4.70	.22	Runoff
6/11/2009	0820	COT	181	4.50	.08	Runoff
7/9/2009	0800	COT	61	4.40	.08	Base flow
8/13/2009	0830	COT	87	4.10	.09	Runoff
11/5/2009	0805	COT	163	4.80	.08	Runoff
12/9/2009	0815	COT	71	4.60	.02	Base flow

[1] Streamflow for data collected by USGS is measured instantaneous streamflow; streamflow for data collected by COT is daily mean streamflow unless streamflow changing rapidly during the day, then it is 15-minute unit value.

[2] Total nitrogen is calculated by adding Kjeldahl-N and nitrite plus nitrate analyses.

[3] Base flow and runoff designated by Base-Flow Index (BFI) program (Institute of Hydrology, 1980a, 1980b).

Appendix 4.   Streamflows, and total nitrogen and total phosphorus concentrations for Spavinaw Creek near Colcord, Oklahoma, 2002–09.

[COT, City of Tulsa; USGS, U.S. Geological Survey; ft³/s, cubic foot per second; mg/L, milligram per liter; N, nitrogen; P, phosphorus; --, not reported; all water-quality and streamflow data available at *http://water.usgs.gov/ok/nwis*]

Date	Sample time	Agency collecting sample	Streamflow[1] (ft³/s)	Total nitrogen concentration (mg/L as N)[2]	Total phosphorus concentration (mg/L as P)	Flow category[3]
1/15/2002	0905	COT	73	5.20	0.11	Base flow
2/1/2002	1706	USGS	388	3.90	.14	Runoff
2/12/2002	0900	COT	113	5.00	.11	Base flow
3/12/2002	0927	COT	132	4.10	.11	Base flow
3/21/2002	1445	USGS	349	4.10	.12	Runoff
4/9/2002	1026	USGS	769	4.10	.13	Runoff
4/18/2002	0902	COT	176	4.40	.13	Base flow
5/13/2002	1342	USGS	269	3.51	.13	Runoff
5/17/2002	1850	USGS	1,670	6.29	.39	Runoff
5/23/2002	0852	COT	210	4.00	.12	Base flow
6/13/2002	0917	COT	168	3.62	.12	Base flow
7/18/2002	0914	COT	58	3.42	.10	Base flow
8/13/2002	0902	COT	36	3.22	.10	Base flow
9/19/2002	0805	COT	22	2.82	.10	Base flow
10/16/2002	0820	COT	21	2.91	.09	Base flow
11/12/2002	0837	COT	33	3.18	.09	Base flow
12/12/2002	0900	COT	34	3.21	.10	Base flow
1/7/2003	0925	COT	59	3.80	.10	Runoff
2/6/2003	0900	COT	30	3.67	.09	Base flow
3/5/2003	0930	COT	113	4.39	.10	Base flow
4/9/2003	0902	COT	61	3.86	.10	Base flow
5/8/2003	0907	COT	48	3.23	.10	Base flow
5/14/2003	0830	COT	61	5.27	.13	Runoff
5/16/2003	1010	COT	467	2.89	.98	Runoff
5/16/2003	1504	USGS	446	3.86	.18	Runoff
5/20/2003	1435	USGS	349	2.30	.28	Runoff
5/21/2003	1607	USGS	446	4.81	.11	Runoff
6/2/2003	1639	USGS	113	4.22	.12	Runoff
6/3/2003	0920	COT	102	3.76	.15	Runoff
6/11/2003	0945	COT	57	3.78	.12	Base flow
6/16/2003	1452	USGS	80	3.69	.11	Runoff
7/10/2003	0841	COT	27	3.23	.09	Base flow
8/5/2003	0845	COT	24	3.01	.09	Base flow
9/2/2003	1418	USGS	88	3.13	.12	Runoff
9/11/2003	0901	COT	44	3.19	.09	Runoff
10/9/2003	0840	COT	23	3.00	.09	Base flow
11/6/2003	0840	COT	23	3.20	.09	Base flow
11/19/2003	1545	USGS	80	3.80	.09	Runoff
12/10/2003	0925	COT	33	3.77	.08	Base flow
1/6/2004	0922	COT	138	4.59	.12	Runoff
1/18/2004	1350	USGS	270	4.50	.10	Runoff
2/5/2004	0850	COT	95	5.05	.09	Base flow
3/4/2004	0909	COT	2,390	5.7	.60	Runoff
3/4/2004	0945	USGS	2,320	6.23	.28	Runoff

Appendix 4. Streamflows, and total nitrogen and total phosphorus concentrations for Spavinaw Creek near Colcord, Oklahoma, 2002–09.—Continued

[COT, City of Tulsa; USGS, U.S. Geological Survey; ft³/s, cubic foot per second; mg/L, milligram per liter; N, nitrogen; P, phosphorus; --, not reported; all water-quality and streamflow data available at *http://water.usgs.gov/ok/nwis*]

Date	Sample time	Agency collecting sample	Streamflow[1] (ft³/s)	Total nitrogen concentration (mg/L as N)[2]	Total phosphorus concentration (mg/L as P)	Flow category[3]
3/29/2004	1600	USGS	646	4.94	0.10	Runoff
4/7/2004	0931	COT	150	4.74	.08	Base flow
4/23/2004	1315	USGS	792	3.32	.10	Runoff
4/24/2004	1235	USGS	4,130	6.08	.99	Runoff
5/6/2004	0904	COT	337	4.62	.09	Runoff
6/10/2004	0900	COT	74	4.37	.09	Base flow
7/3/2004	1405	USGS	7,200	3.54	.94	Runoff
7/8/2004	0910	COT	424	4.51	.09	Runoff
8/5/2004	0910	COT	172	3.98	.15	Base flow
9/9/2004	0910	COT	69	4.04	.11	Base flow
10/7/2004	0845	COT	34	3.81	.08	Base flow
11/1/2004	1730	USGS	1,280	4.68	.19	Runoff
11/3/2004	0935	COT	397	4.70	.13	Runoff
12/9/2004	0927	COT	374	5.03	.08	Runoff
1/5/2005	1430	USGS	5,700	9.62	1.10	Runoff
1/6/2005	0945	COT	2,190	5.54	.23	Runoff
2/10/2005	0917	COT	155	5.18	.08	Base flow
3/10/2005	0920	COT	129	4.59	.08	Base flow
4/7/2005	0928	COT	296	3.90	.09	Runoff
5/12/2005	0907	COT	84	4.07	.11	Base flow
6/9/2005	0950	COT	47	3.64	.08	Base flow
6/15/2005	1350	USGS	90	3.63	.15	Runoff
7/14/2005	0915	COT	34	2.90	.09	Base flow
8/11/2005	0850	COT	30	3.02	.08	Base flow
9/15/2005	0925	COT	21	2.90	.07	Base flow
10/6/2005	0900	COT	19	3.06	.08	Base flow
11/16/2005	0845	COT	27	3.46	.07	Base flow
12/15/2005	0857	COT	21	3.55	.07	Base flow
1/12/2006	0855	COT	21	3.64	.26	Base flow
2/9/2006	0913	COT	22	3.61	.08	Base flow
3/9/2006	0850	COT	30	3.32	.07	Base flow
4/12/2006	0850	USGS	34	2.94	--	Runoff
4/29/2006	1355	USGS	68	2.67	.10	Runoff
5/2/2006	1410	USGS	153	3.41	.09	Runoff
5/10/2006	0917	COT	142	3.18	.10	Runoff
5/10/2006	1150	USGS	191	3.41	.13	Runoff
6/8/2006	0925	COT	39	--[4]	.10	Runoff
7/13/2006	0947	COT	13	--[4]	.07	Base flow
7/13/2006	1300	USGS	12	2.47	.07	Base flow
8/10/2006	0842	USGS	11	2.28	--	Base flow
8/28/2006	1345	USGS	30	2.08	.07	Runoff
9/14/2006	0927	USGS	29	3.01	--	Base flow
10/12/2006	0926	COT	15	3.07	--	Base flow
11/16/2006	0815	COT	24	2.94	--	Base flow

Appendix 4.   Streamflows, and total nitrogen and total phosphorus concentrations for Spavinaw Creek near Colcord, Oklahoma, 2002–09.—Continued

[COT, City of Tulsa; USGS, U.S. Geological Survey; ft³/s, cubic foot per second; mg/L, milligram per liter; N, nitrogen; P, phosphorus; --, not reported; all water-quality and streamflow data available at *http://water.usgs.gov/ok/nwis*]

Date	Sample time	Agency collecting sample	Streamflow[1] (ft³/s)	Total nitrogen concentration (mg/L as N)[2]	Total phosphorus concentration (mg/L as P)	Flow category[3]
12/6/2006	0940	COT	132	5.03	--	Runoff
1/11/2007	1002	COT	82	5.44	0.07	Base flow
1/23/2007	1600	USGS	306	5.69	.09	Runoff
2/8/2007	0945	COT	99	5.84	.08	Base flow
3/7/2007	0938	COT	88	5.01	.07	Base flow
4/19/2007	0942	COT	90	3.79	.08	Runoff
5/7/2007	1410	USGS	329	3.14	.35	Runoff
5/8/2007	0918	COT	325	3.12	.12	Runoff
5/8/2007	1320	USGS	311	3.17	.24	Runoff
5/29/2007	1245	USGS	57	2.68	.04	Base flow
6/7/2007	0910	COT	43	3.01	.07	Base flow
6/12/2007	1445	USGS	700	8.11	1.50	Runoff
6/13/2007	1315	USGS	199	2.73	.10	Runoff
6/18/2007	1030	USGS	82	3.02	.08	Runoff
7/12/2007	0918	COT	53	2.60	.06	Base flow
7/24/2007	1000	USGS	37	2.38	.06	Base flow
8/2/2007	1330	USGS	28	2.20	.07	Base flow
8/9/2007	0900	COT	21	2.25	.07	Base flow
9/10/2007	1315	USGS	187	3.36	.10	Runoff
9/13/2007	0930	COT	129	3.37	.07	Runoff
10/2/2007	1045	USGS	57	3.10	.11	Runoff
10/3/2007	1200	USGS	741	5.24	.24	Runoff
10/11/2007	0930	COT	132	4.90	.09	Runoff
10/18/2007	1200	USGS	90	4.50	.09	Base flow
11/8/2007	0855	COT	53	4.50	.08	Base flow
12/11/2007	1400	USGS	564	5.10	.12	Runoff
12/18/2007	1255	COT	239	6.10	.06	Runoff
1/8/2008	1000	USGS	5,520	7.58	.90	Runoff
1/17/2008	1000	COT	195	6.20	.08	Runoff
2/14/2008	0935	COT	206	5.00	.07	Runoff
2/17/2008	1100	USGS	3,470	6.00	.71	Runoff
3/3/2008	1100	USGS	2,180	5.10	.25	Runoff
3/12/2008	0940	COT	187	5.40	.06	Runoff
3/18/2008	1445	USGS	9,620	6.22	1.60	Runoff
4/1/2008	1000	USGS	1,100	3.80	.12	Runoff
4/16/2008	0935	COT	404	4.20	.08	Base flow
5/7/2008	0935	COT	184	3.80	.06	Base flow
6/10/2008	1400	USGS	1,780	3.26	.16	Runoff
6/12/2008	0950	COT	585	3.60	.09	Runoff
7/16/2008	0923	COT	321	3.70	.07	Runoff
8/14/2008	0950	COT	137	3.70	.08	Runoff
9/5/2008	1200	USGS	305	3.80	.08	Runoff
9/11/2008	0930	COT	137	4.00	.08	Base flow
9/14/2008	1245	USGS	2,060	4.02	.33	Runoff

Appendix 4.   Streamflows, and total nitrogen and total phosphorus concentrations for Spavinaw Creek near Colcord, Oklahoma, 2002–09.—Continued

[COT, City of Tulsa; USGS, U.S. Geological Survey; ft³/s, cubic foot per second; mg/L, milligram per liter; N, nitrogen; P, phosphorus; --, not reported; all water-quality and streamflow data available at *http://water.usgs.gov/ok/nwis*]

Date	Sample time	Agency collecting sample	Streamflow[1] (ft³/s)	Total nitrogen concentration (mg/L as N)[2]	Total phosphorus concentration (mg/L as P)	Flow category[3]
10/9/2008	0950	COT	98	4.20	0.08	Base flow
11/6/2008	0930	COT	68	4.20	.07	Base flow
12/11/2008	1005	COT	54	4.10	.07	Base flow
1/8/2009	1010	COT	73	4.30	.07	Runoff
2/11/2009	1215	USGS	471	4.45	.24	Runoff
2/12/2009	0945	COT	809	4.99	.09	Runoff
3/5/2009	0910	COT	88	4.40	.06	Base flow
3/30/2009	1245	USGS	382	3.90	.06	Runoff
4/16/2009	0940	COT	366	4.10	.06	Runoff
5/4/2009	1045	USGS	1,250	4.13	.08	Runoff
5/8/2009	1620	USGS	1,300	4.97	.19	Runoff
5/14/2009	0940	COT	570	4.30	.28	Runoff
6/11/2009	0940	COT	233	4.20	.07	Runoff
7/9/2009	0930	COT	75	3.90	.06	Base flow
8/13/2009	0950	COT	108	3.60	.07	Runoff
9/10/2009	0930	COT	181	3.12	.24	Runoff
9/10/2009	1515	USGS	125	2.70	.10	Runoff
9/22/2009	1045	USGS	509	3.73	.18	Runoff
10/8/2009	0830	COT	55	3.90	.08	Runoff
10/9/2009	1630	USGS	5,760	5.29	.83	Runoff
11/5/2009	0930	COT	268	4.85	.08	Runoff
12/9/2009	0950	COT	96	4.30	.07	Base flow

[1] Streamflow for data collected by USGS is measured instantaneous streamflow; streamflow for data collected by COT is daily mean streamflow unless streamflow changing rapidly during the day, then it is 15-minute unit value.

[2] Total nitrogen is calculated by adding Kjeldahl-N and nitrite plus nitrate analyses.

[3] Base flow and runoff designated by Base-Flow Index (BFI) program (Institute of Hydrology, 1980a, 1980b).

[4] Nitrite plus nitrate analyses not reported, nitrate analyses were substituted in the total nitrogen calculation for this sample.

Appendix 5. Streamflows, and total nitrogen and total phosphorus concentrations for Beaty Creek near Jay, Oklahoma, 2002–09.

[COT, City of Tulsa; USGS, U.S. Geological Survey; ft³/s, cubic foot per second; mg/L, milligram per liter; N, nitrogen; P, phosphorus; --, not reported; all water-quality and streamflow data available at *http://water.usgs.gov/ok/nwis*]

Date	Sample time	Agency collecting sample	Streamflow[1] (ft³/s)	Total nitrogen concentration (mg/L as N)[2]	Total phosphorus concentration (mg/L as P)	Flow category[3]
1/15/2002	0940	COT	10	3.20	0.04	Base flow
2/1/2002	1911	USGS	99	2.60	.05	Runoff
2/12/2002	0755	COT	25	3.20	.03	Runoff
3/12/2002	0750	COT	33	2.70	.03	Runoff
4/8/2002	1837	USGS	189	3.60	.15	Runoff
4/18/2002	0752	COT	29	2.90	.04	Runoff
5/17/2002	1220	USGS	231	3.98	.17	Runoff
5/23/2002	0805	COT	54	2.80	.05	Runoff
5/28/2002	1542	USGS	519	4.68	.81	Runoff
6/13/2002	0735	COT	58	2.57	.05	Runoff
7/18/2002	0742	COT	7.2	2.27	.03	Base flow
8/13/2002	0820	COT	1.8	1.45	.05	Base flow
9/19/2002	0755	COT	0	1.15	.05	Base flow
10/16/2002	0800	COT	.1	1.24	.04	Base flow
11/12/2002	0920	COT	2.8	1.34	.03	Base flow
12/12/2002	0755	COT	4.4	1.34	.03	Base flow
1/7/2003	0750	COT	7.2	1.79	.04	Base flow
2/6/2003	0755	COT	3.9	1.53	.02	Base flow
3/5/2003	0735	COT	39	2.93	.02	Runoff
4/9/2003	0720	COT	17	2.16	.03	Base flow
5/8/2003	0725	COT	12	1.53	.04	Base flow
5/14/2003	0850	COT	26	2.01	.04	Runoff
5/16/2003	1048	COT	127	1.41	.08	Runoff
5/16/2003	1741	USGS	414	3.27	.15	Runoff
5/20/2003	1929	USGS	263	3.60	.28	Runoff
5/21/2003	1743	USGS	135	3.01	.07	Runoff
6/2/2003	1755	USGS	118	3.78	.06	Runoff
6/3/2003	0730	COT	108	2.30	.04	Runoff
6/11/2003	1000	COT	22	2.27	.04	Runoff
6/26/2003	1044	USGS	12	1.87	.04	Runoff
7/10/2003	0750	COT	7.5	1.85	.03	Base flow
8/5/2003	0730	COT	.4	1.62	.04	Base flow
9/2/2003	1549	USGS	15	1.13	.04	Runoff
9/11/2003	0727	COT	3.0	.87	.03	Base flow
10/9/2003	0705	COT	4.0	.93	.03	Base flow
11/6/2003	0730	COT	6.4	1.00	.04	Base flow
11/19/2003	1722	USGS	15	1.51	.03	Runoff
12/10/2003	0750	COT	6.7	2.26	.03	Base flow
1/6/2004	0735	COT	26	2.58	.03	Runoff
1/18/2004	1205	USGS	212	3.45	.11	Runoff
2/5/2004	0725	COT	25	4.02	.03	Base flow
3/4/2004	0744	COT	1,350	4.93	.96	Runoff
3/4/2004	1345	USGS	916	4.13	.26	Runoff
3/29/2004	1720	USGS	346	3.39	.09	Runoff

Appendix 5. Streamflows, and total nitrogen and total phosphorus concentrations for Beaty Creek near Jay, Oklahoma, 2002–09.— Continued

[COT, City of Tulsa; USGS, U.S. Geological Survey; ft³/s, cubic foot per second; mg/L, milligram per liter; N, nitrogen; P, phosphorus; --, not reported; all water-quality and streamflow data available at *http://water.usgs.gov/ok/nwis*]

Date	Sample time	Agency collecting sample	Streamflow[1] (ft³/s)	Total nitrogen concentration (mg/L as N)[2]	Total phosphorus concentration (mg/L as P)	Flow category[3]
4/7/2004	0729	COT	29	3.42	0.04	Base flow
4/23/2004	1115	USGS	162	2.66	.08	Runoff
4/24/2004	1030	USGS	1,080	3.28	.46	Runoff
5/6/2004	0724	COT	186	3.32	.05	Runoff
6/10/2004	0720	COT	20	2.66	.05	Base flow
7/3/2004	1635	USGS	953	2.67	.49	Runoff
7/8/2004	0720	COT	104	3.16	.07	Runoff
8/5/2004	0729	COT	18	2.57	.09	Base flow
9/9/2004	0718	COT	7.1	2.20	.05	Base flow
10/7/2004	0720	COT	4.0	1.84	.05	Base flow
11/1/2004	1120	USGS	2,050	4.24	1.0	Runoff
11/3/2004	0738	COT	181	3.05	.10	Runoff
12/9/2004	0740	COT	144	3.67	.08	Runoff
1/6/2005	0720	COT	603	4.11	.27	Runoff
1/13/2005	1325	USGS	486	3.50	.23	Runoff
2/10/2005	0730	COT	48	3.78	.04	Base flow
3/10/2005	0730	COT	25	3.13	.04	Base flow
4/7/2005	0735	COT	142	3.28	.07	Runoff
5/12/2005	0625	COT	15	2.58	.06	Base flow
6/9/2005	0755	COT	10	2.07	.05	Base flow
6/14/2005	1030	USGS	85	1.89	.07	Runoff
7/14/2005	0725	COT	4.0	1.47	.06	Base flow
8/11/2005	0735	COT	.6	.89	.04	Base flow
9/15/2005	0755	COT	.1	.88	.07	Base flow
10/6/2005	0745	COT	0	.99	.05	Base flow
11/16/2005	0734	COT	2.8	1.16	.04	Base flow
12/15/2005	0750	COT	1.7	1.18	.03	Base flow
1/12/2006	0740	COT	2.1	1.37	.10	Base flow
2/9/2006	0905	COT	1.7	1.21	.03	Base flow
3/9/2006	0806	COT	2.6	1.45	.03	Base flow
4/12/2006	0738	COT	2.1	1.04	--	Base flow
4/29/2006	1210	USGS	26	1.16	.04	Runoff
5/2/2006	1125	USGS	35	1.57	.03	Runoff
5/10/2006	0810	COT	535	2.70	.23	Runoff
5/10/2006	1030	USGS	519	3.11	.21	Runoff
6/8/2006	0745	COT	7.5	--[4]	.04	Base flow
7/13/2006	0735	COT	0	--[4]	.06	Base flow
8/29/2006	1125	USGS	19	1.77	.05	Runoff
9/14/2006	0745	COT	2.8	.67	--	Base flow
11/16/2006	0835	COT	.7	.91	--	Base flow
12/6/2006	0745	COT	32	3.47	--	Runoff
1/11/2007	0800	COT	16	4.07	.05	Base flow
1/23/2007	1130	USGS	159	4.02	.10	Runoff
2/8/2007	0750	COT	10	4.29	.04	Runoff

Appendix 5.   Streamflows, and total nitrogen and total phosphorus concentrations for Beaty Creek near Jay, Oklahoma, 2002–09.—
Continued

[COT, City of Tulsa; USGS, U.S. Geological Survey; ft³/s, cubic foot per second; mg/L, milligram per liter; N, nitrogen; P, phosphorus; --, not reported; all
water-quality and streamflow data available at *http://water.usgs.gov/ok/nwis*]

Date	Sample time	Agency collecting sample	Streamflow[1] (ft³/s)	Total nitrogen concentration (mg/L as N)[2]	Total phosphorus concentration (mg/L as P)	Flow category[3]
3/7/2007	0755	COT	8.3	3.28	0.04	Base flow
4/19/2007	0754	COT	10	2.06	.04	Runoff
5/7/2007	1217	USGS	22	1.57	.04	Runoff
5/7/2007	1635	USGS	258	2.66	.21	Runoff
5/8/2007	0745	COT	406	3.58	.12	Runoff
5/8/2007	1500	USGS	355	2.88	.18	Runoff
5/29/2007	1330	USGS	21	2.70	.04	Runoff
6/7/2007	0800	COT	6.5	2.41	.04	Base flow
6/12/2007	1645	USGS	950	5.12	.89	Runoff
6/13/2007	1120	USGS	390	2.54	.13	Runoff
6/18/2007	1215	USGS	76	2.53	.06	Runoff
7/12/2007	0750	COT	12	1.81	.05	Runoff
7/24/2007	1130	USGS	9.1	1.54	.04	Base flow
8/2/2007	1530	USGS	27	1.70	.05	Runoff
8/9/2007	0800	COT	3.5	1.62	.05	Base flow
9/12/2007	1200	USGS	18	1.26	.05	Runoff
9/13/2007	0735	COT	12	1.30	.06	Runoff
10/2/2007	1325	USGS	37	1.70	.06	Runoff
10/3/2007	1020	USGS	738	3.50	.44	Runoff
10/11/2007	0742	COT	66	3.10	.05	Runoff
11/8/2007	0740	COT	37	3.40	.05	Base flow
12/11/2007	1210	USGS	429	3.50	.18	Runoff
12/18/2007	1015	COT	239	4.60	.06	Runoff
1/8/2008	1645	USGS	1,045	4.69	.58	Runoff
1/17/2008	0755	COT	197	5.00	.06	Runoff
2/14/2008	0735	COT	263	3.75	.06	Runoff
2/17/2008	1100	COT	675	3.78	.44	Runoff
3/3/2008	1230	USGS	811	3.70	.38	Runoff
3/12/2008	0730	COT	112	4.10	.05	Base flow
4/16/2008	0720	COT	139	3.40	.07	Base flow
5/7/2008	0722	COT	64	3.10	.05	Runoff
6/10/2008	1200	USGS	685	2.12	.20	Runoff
6/12/2008	0735	COT	263	2.80	.10	Runoff
7/16/2008	0730	COT	38	2.50	.06	Runoff
8/14/2008	0741	COT	60	2.80	.07	Runoff
9/5/2008	1037	USGS	51	2.60	.07	Runoff
9/11/2008	0728	COT	18	2.60	.06	Base flow
9/14/2008	1030	USGS	1,710	3.25	.52	Runoff
10/9/2008	0748	COT	22	3.00	.06	Base flow
11/6/2008	0725	COT	21	2.70	.05	Base flow
12/11/2008	0940	COT	19	2.50	.06	Runoff
1/8/2009	0803	COT	14	3.34	.05	Runoff
2/11/2009	1045	USGS	464	4.22	.27	Runoff
2/12/2009	0740	COT	333	3.70	.14	Runoff

Appendix 5.   Streamflows, and total nitrogen and total phosphorus concentrations for Beaty Creek near Jay, Oklahoma, 2002–09.—
Continued

[COT, City of Tulsa; USGS, U.S. Geological Survey; ft³/s, cubic foot per second; mg/L, milligram per liter; N, nitrogen; P, phosphorus; --, not reported; all
water-quality and streamflow data available at *http://water.usgs.gov/ok/nwis*]

Date	Sample time	Agency collecting sample	Streamflow[1] (ft³/s)	Total nitrogen concentration (mg/L as N)[2]	Total phosphorus concentration (mg/L as P)	Flow category[3]
3/5/2009	0710	COT	15	3.00	0.05	Base flow
3/30/2009	1100	USGS	117	2.40	.06	Runoff
4/16/2009	0735	COT	86	2.70	.06	Runoff
5/4/2009	0930	USGS	344	2.50	.10	Runoff
5/8/2009	1445	USGS	758	7.27	1.10	Runoff
5/14/2009	0733	COT	113	3.50	.11	Runoff
6/11/2009	0723	COT	55	3.00	.09	Runoff
7/9/2009	0710	COT	13	2.80	.05	Base flow
8/13/2009	0730	COT	21	2.30	.07	Runoff
9/10/2009	0720	COT	386	2.77	.26	Runoff
9/10/2009	1350	USGS	216	2.51	.16	Runoff
9/22/2009	1040	USGS	662	2.83	.50	Runoff
10/8/2009	0704	COT	22	2.90	.13	Runoff
10/9/2009	1400	USGS	3,040	2.99	.86	Runoff
11/5/2009	0715	COT	92	3.46	.07	Runoff
12/9/2009	0710	COT	26	3.00	.06	Base flow

[1] Streamflow for data collected by USGS is measured instantaneous streamflow; streamflow for data collected by COT is daily mean streamflow unless streamflow changing rapidly during the day, then it is 15-minute unit value.

[2] Total nitrogen is calculated by adding Kjeldahl-N and nitrite plus nitrate analyses.

[3] Base flow and runoff designated by Base-Flow Index (BFI) program (Institute of Hydrology, 1980a, 1980b).

[4] Nitrite plus nitrate analyses not reported, nitrate analyses were substituted in the total nitrogen calculation for this sample.